BRIDGE BUILDERS

"If you rely on relationship-building to make a living, read this book! *Bridge Builders* will entice you to examine your obstacles and equip you with the practical tools to overcome them."

—**Peri Shawn,** Leadership Coach;
Award-Winning Author of *Sell More with Sales Coaching*

"Finding the right talent is still a problem for organizations looking to fill key positions. Companies are desperately looking for *top quality* candidates who fit the culture and can immediately begin solving challenges. Maria's *Bridge Builders: How Superb Communicators Get What They Want* offers an insightful look at the type of candidates who will stand out in today's increasingly competitive market."

—**Will Gowin,** President of
Spencer Gray, Inc. | A Staffing Solutions Company

"In my 20+ years experience helping build, grow, and monetize new companies I know that building bridges to investors and stakeholders is mission-critical. If your dream and vision depend on someone saying, "Yes," do yourself a favor: read, learn, and put into practice the five principles in *Bridge Builders.*"

—**J.D. Davids**, Entrepreneur and Founder of The Fronis Group

"Solving the most prevalent HR problems today always seems to boil down to resolving communication and leadership issues. Maria Keckler gets to the heart of what it takes to do just that. I highly recommend that entire teams read this book together!"

—**Julia Vaughn**, Director of Benefits and
Risk Management, Shadow Mountain Ministries

"I'm impressed with the inherent wisdom and practicality of Maria's work. Don't wait! Take the ideas and run with them for the sake of your relationships, your career, and your goals."

—**Lisa Gates**, Communication and Leadership Specialist,
University of California, San Diego

"*Bridge Builders* is a brilliant, practical book that will teach you how to improve communication and leadership skills when it really counts. But Maria goes deeper than mere instructions. This book is ultimately about discovering what keeps you from achieving your dreams and goals and then developing the mindset that will enable you to move others to join your vision."

—**Carolyn Konecki,** Vice President,
Leavitt Insurance Agency of San Diego, Inc.

"The value of clear and effective communication is often overlooked and even dismissed within organizations. Maria shows us what a mistake this is by illustrating how being a strong communicator—a bridge builder—provides a path to achieving your goals, both professionally and personally."

—**Brad Parker,** Director of Marketing at Sony Electronics

"Wow! I cannot remember a more interesting and well-written book designed to improve communication and living a richer life—personally and professionally. Awesome! I could use this immediately."

—**Valda Boyd Ford**, CEO and Founder of
Center for Human Diversity

"I never expected to be so personally affected by a book aimed at improving my business communication skills. This book can be transformational if you let it."

—**Thomas Varallo**, Commander, U.S. Navy (Retired)

"Coaching leaders and employees to success is by far one of the greatest investments a company can make to gain a competitive advantage. *Bridge Builders* delivers the why and the how."

—**Donna Evans**, Founder and CEO of Team Building for Success

"Innovative, insightful, intriguing and inspiring! Maria Keckler's *Bridge Builders* will help you prevent or reverse the damage of ineffective leadership and poor communication—if you read it and apply the principles immediately."

—**Bill and Pam Farrel**, International speakers; bestselling authors of *Men Are Like Waffles, Women Are Like Spaghetti*; co-founders of Love-Wise

"Maria Keckler shares an unusual gift with this book. I recommend it to every ambitious leader, type A individual, and to anyone who wants to effectively lead a team and get outstanding results in business or in life."

—**Caxton Opere**, MD, CEO, Koth Clinic Inc.

"Powerfully insightful! *Bridge Builders* will equip you with the right tools to get from where you are, to where you inspire to be. Learn the value and power of your own life's stories as you read about Daniel's transformation. This book is a must read for anyone who has important goals to reach."

—**Mishe Serra**, Chief Strategy Officer, K2 Design and Strategy

"*Bridge Builders* provides useful insights for navigating our highly competitive society. Parents, college hopefuls, and soon-to-be college graduates can get ahead of the game by reading this book."

—**Pamela Donnelly**, #1 bestselling author of *SWAT Team Tactics for Getting Your Teen Into College* and *4 Keys to College Admissions Success*

BRIDGE BUILDERS

How Superb Communicators
Get What They Want
in Business and in Life

MARIA KECKLER

New York

BRIDGE BUILDERS

How Superb Communicators Get What They Want in Business and in Life

© 2016 MARIA KECKLER.

Published in New York, New York, by Morgan James Publishing. Morgan James and The Entrepreneurial Publisher are trademarks of Morgan James, LLC. www.MorganJamesPublishing.com

The Morgan James Speakers Group can bring authors to your live event. For more information or to book an event visit The Morgan James Speakers Group at www.TheMorganJamesSpeakersGroup.com.

A **free** eBook edition is available with the purchase of this print book.

CLEARLY PRINT YOUR NAME ABOVE IN UPPER CASE

Instructions to claim your free eBook edition:
1. Download the BitLit app for Android or iOS
2. Write your name in **UPPER CASE** on the line
3. Use the BitLit app to submit a photo
4. Download your eBook to any device

ISBN 978-1-63047-539-0 paperback
ISBN 978-1-63047-540-6 eBook
ISBN 978-1-63047-541-3 hardcover
Library of Congress Control Number: 2014959670

Cover Design by:
Rachel Lopez
www.r2cdesign.com

In an effort to support local communities and raise awareness and funds, Morgan James Publishing donates a percentage of all book sales for the life of each book to Habitat for Humanity Peninsula and Greater Williamsburg.

Get involved today, visit
www.MorganJamesBuilds.com

Habitat for Humanity®
Peninsula and Greater Williamsburg
Building Partner

To Sam and Sarah,
my favorite Bridge Builders.

TABLE OF CONTENTS

FOREWORD

By Dr. David Jeremiah

The day before I met Maria, I received a call from our new Chief Technology Officer whose first task was to usher the academic institutions in our organization into the 21st century by the end of the summer.

Selecting and purchasing state-of-the-art technology was the easy part. Getting employees to embrace it by radically changing the way they planned and delivered teaching and training—that was the challenge.

If we were going to be successful, we needed someone who could help bridge the gap between our technical staff (the IT folks who installed and supported the technology) and the end users (the educators who would need to learn it and adopt it).

We needed someone who could advocate both for our technical staff (when things didn't work the way they were supposed to) and for our non-technical users (when frustration made them want to quit).

We didn't know it at the time, but what we needed was a Bridge Builder. And that's what we got when Maria joined the team. In only two years, not only had we reached our short-term and long-term goals, we had also become a model for other institutions that reached out to us. They wanted to know how we were able to go from almost zero academic technology to over 85 percent adoption in such a short period of time. Maria's answer: one bridge at a time. She discusses this journey in more detail in the "Case for Bridge Builder Cultures" chapter.

If you've just opened this book not knowing what to expect, you're in for a treat. Maria has written an important parable and shared principles that can transform your professional and personal life. *Bridge Builders: How Superb Communicators Get What They Want in Business and in Life* will challenge the way you think about yourself and your ability to reach your goals.

My advice: Before you jump to the "how-to" section of the book, do yourself a favor and read the story from beginning to end. Read it more than once. Read it with your team. Take the time to reflect on the discussion questions. You may just find that Daniel's story is your story as well.

Thanks, Maria!

—**Dr. David Jeremiah**, Founder, Turning Point Radio
and Turning Point Television Ministries,
International bestselling author of *What Are You Afraid Of?*

FOREWORD

By Kathrine Kimball

We can easily spend our entire careers building diverse, technical toolkits yet the ability to truly express mutual value in a relationship trumps all else. Intentional communication is the only tool that has unlimited potential.

Having worked in international business for over twenty years, I have experienced the power of "Bridge Building" in transcending strategic cultural barriers while minimizing the logistical challenges of operating in a global team. At the same time, I have seen how the void of strong relationships can guarantee failure.

In *Bridge Builders: How Superb Communicators Get What They Want in Business and in Life*, Maria illustrates that becoming a Bridge Builder is possible for anyone who is willing to abandon preconceived ideas and avoid the common pitfalls that keep us from truly connecting to others.

Allow Maria's timeless principles and life lessons around "Superb" communication to renew your enthusiasm for investing in others, whether you are shifting gears to move to the next level in your career, or a younger professional setting your stage. Presented in a creatively-woven parable, Maria's threads of wisdom bring a new perspective to how I will be re-prioritizing communication with my clients and colleagues as well as my family and friends. A few of Maria's priceless threads that resonated with me are:

- The transformation to becoming a Bridge Builder is not about perfection; it's about intention and making a choice to put the needs of others before your own.
- "Critics are all around us;" they attempt to predict our successes as well as our failures. Be authentic and feel confident in knowing that what truly matters is what you think coupled with your own actions and reactions.
- Maria reminds us to listen not just with our ears, but also with our eyes, our mind, and our heart. As a beloved professor shared, the key to success is to develop both a "compassionate mind and an intelligent heart."
- Story. Usefulness. Passion. Empathy. Reliability. Brevity. These are the SUPERB tools that belong in the Bridge Builder's toolbox. Using them strategically and intentionally—whether you're delivering a presentation, facilitating a meeting, making a personal connection, or getting the recognition you have earned—will set you apart.
- You too have a Bridge Builder story that can radically transform the way you lead yourself and others. Write your story. Hone your story. Tell your story. Listen to the stories of others.

We have all spent time and energy repairing bridges that have crumbled due to careless communication. Imagine what would happen if we spent more time building and strengthening bridges to the hearts and minds of the people we want to reach with our message.

Simply by opening this book, you are inviting the possibility of developing stronger, mutually valuable relationships. Be intentional. Be authentic. Be passionate. Be superb.

—**Kathrine Kimball**, Bridge Builder; Vision San Diego, CFO; Wife of 26 years (not bad for a blind date!) and Mother of two children who will change their world with their compassionate minds and intelligent hearts~

INTRODUCTION

An extraordinary desire drives you. You have a story to tell. You have a product, service, idea, or vision to sell—at home or at work. How you choose to communicate your message and connect with your target audience will make the difference between success and failure.

When you make a decision to communicate your message like a Bridge Builder, you will achieve more of what you want. You'll be a Superb Communicator who is able to persuade audiences—

To listen. To engage. To connect.
To buy your products.
To join your causes.
To approve your initiatives.
To fund your ideas.
To believe in your vision.
To let you lead.

The premise of this book is simple: You already know how to be a Bridge Builder—although you may not realize it. Like most people, you've probably forgotten. But you've successfully built bridges before. Intention, not perfection, helped you achieve what you wanted. And intention, not perfection, will help you achieve what you want in the future. When you *choose* to operate from the principles illustrated in the story and in the approach that follows it, the results will amaze you.

Getting the Most From the Story

Stories often are used to communicate important principles. Why? Because we all relate to life through stories. We see aspects of ourselves in the characters, and we hope to gain new insights about business and life from the way they react and the things they learn in the story.

The parable in this book is about a man named Daniel who, like us, has a problem (how to communicate effectively with others), but doesn't recognize the source of his problem or how to solve it. Daniel needs to become a Bridge Builder in order to get what he truly wants; but he struggles to accept the solution to his problem because of past failure, preconceptions, and misunderstandings. He exemplifies the individuals I encounter every day in one-to-one coaching and the corporate consulting process.

The characters in this story represent composites of real business professionals I've worked with, not anyone in particular. However, early feedback from readers who represent varied industries and cultures tells me that the characters and themes in the story will resonate with most readers in more ways than one.

This story applies to business communication, but it also applies to communication at home, at school, at church, and in any organizational setting. Because the story deals with communication and leadership principles, anyone will benefit from reading it, whether or not they work in the corporate world.

Organizations, large or small, also will reap the profits of intentionally nurturing a culture of Bridge Builder Communication and

Bridge Builder Leadership—and so will those inside these organizations, whether they're executives, scientists, engineers, sales reps, entrepreneurs, educators, pastors, fundraisers, or creatives. That has been my experience.

I suggest that you first read and reflect on the story. Then take the time to ask questions that are naturally suggested in the narrative.

- Should I explore a new approach to how I communicate and deal with others?
- Are my preconceived ideas or attitudes toward communication and leadership holding me back—at home or at work?
- What people in my life model effective communication and leadership?
- What is holding me back from becoming a more effective communicator and leader?
- What does it mean to engage the hearts and minds of my audiences?
- What am I afraid of?
- What if I stopped being afraid . . . ?

Additionally, I have included a brief section at the end of each chapter, Bridge Builder Notes, to help you reflect on at least one meaningful concept.

If you prefer to read through a story uninterrupted, like I do, you can skip the Bridge Builder Notes and return to them later. If you are reading and discussing the book with your team or as part of a reading group, the Bridge Builder Notes will jump-start meaningful conversation. And if you want more in-depth discussion questions, you can download them from the Book's Resources Website.

By investing time in reading this book and engaging the process, you have set yourself apart. Consider the following words by George Bernard Shaw. In a single sentence, he voiced the communication deficit that sets Bridge Builders apart from the rest of the crowd: "The biggest problem with communication is the illusion that it has taken place."

Bottom line—far too many people are satisfied with ordinary communication. This is the reason successful organizations are desperately looking for communicators and leaders who can build bridges to others. Today, you can join those who choose to raise the bar, to achieve their goals, and to inspire others to do the same.

Let's get started.

Book's Resource Website
LeadersBuildBridges.com

PART I
THE PARABLE

"If a man will begin with certainties, he shall end in doubts; but if he will be content to begin with doubts, he shall end in certainties."
—**Francis Bacon**

Five days ago.

CHAPTER 1

THE GIFT

Son,

If you are reading this letter, it is because you have accepted the board's challenge to prove that you are the man to write the next chapter for BeyondYou . . . and what I feared most has happened—that you and I didn't have time to repair the bridge of communication that crumbled between us. This is my deepest regret. I don't blame you. Please don't blame yourself.

As you know, I, too, lost my father early in life. More than once I wished he had left me with one last piece of advice to help me navigate an uncertain future. Sensing that my time may be cut short, I want to do that for you, Daniel.

A mentor once told me that it is almost as presumptuous to think you can do nothing as to think you can do everything. The advice has served me well.

Not money. Not power. Not the greatest product. Not shrewd business savvy. Not even talent, timing, or intelligence fueled my success. People who were willing to join and follow my leadership have always been the fuel.

I was blessed to have people who invested their hearts and souls in the BeyondYou vision. This same gift can be yours, too, if you remember how to build bridges to people's minds and hearts.

I was also blessed to have a mentor to show me how. The Bridge Builder, the friend and mentor I met when I was just a fledgling entrepreneur with nothing but a dream and fear of failure, can help you too.

How I wish I could see you rediscover the man you were born to be. How I wish I had more time to share all I want to say, Son. But I leave you with the next best thing—a special gift that will deliver what I am not able to share with you. I have asked Paul to arrange all the details in my absence. I hope you will accept it.

With all my love,
Dad

Daniel folded the letter and slid it into the inner pocket of his suit jacket. He closed his eyes and pondered the words yet another time, as if he were trying to solve a riddle. No matter how hard he'd drilled Paul, the vice chair of BeyondYou's board, hoping to get answers, his father's loyal friend had remained unmoved. Neither Daniel's perplexity about what his father meant about building bridges nor his incensed demand that Paul tell him why he had to meet a mysterious stranger first thing Monday morning to receive the "special gift" had yielded the answers he wanted.

Paul had left Daniel's office with only a firm pat on the back and words that would haunt Daniel for the next few days: "Consider this gift your father's last official decision as CEO. When you return and take your seat at the helm of BeyondYou, you'll have time enough to live with the decisions you make. Go home to pack; your plane leaves in three hours."

Bridge Builder Notes

It has been said that art imitates life, and so is the case with Daniel's story. His father's letter is the inciting incident—a catalyst occurrence—that sets a series of life-changing events in motion, forcing him to take action.

- What inciting incidents are taking place in your personal or professional life right now?
- Are you willing to join Daniel's journey and discover what's in it for you?

CHAPTER 2

THE CRITICS

Daniel searched his pants pockets, but found only two wrinkled pieces of paper he'd been carrying all week—the letter that had set the last five days in motion and the article he'd read more times than he cared to admit. Behind him, he heard Chris's cell phone ring. Daniel stuck the folded letter back into his pocket and unfolded the worn newspaper article as his father's mentor answered her call.

"Okay, we'll be down in five minutes."

"Well, it looks like we're really finally about to find out," he muttered to himself as he rubbed the creases.

"What's that?" She clicked off her phone and slid it into the purse she'd placed on the corner of her desk.

He handed her the article. "Last week's article from the Times."

BeyondYou, Inc. May Be Sailing without a Rudder

Daniel Reed, Jr., will stand as interim CEO of BeyondYou, Inc.—despite heavy criticism from the tech world—following the untimely death of his father and BeyondYou's founder, CEO, and chairman of the board. Mr. Reed died of complications from heart surgery Tuesday morning. He was 57.

Mr. Reed, Sr., led the way for BeyondYou to become one of the most innovative and prolific telecommunication companies based in Silicon Valley. Under his leadership, BeyondYou has dominated the industry for almost two decades. Friends and peers say he was "the heart and soul" of the company.

Known for his extraordinary communication skills, Reed, Sr., is credited for working side by side with strategic partners, investors, and employees, changing the face of Silicon Valley's corporate culture and privately-owned business practices. He leaves very big shoes to fill.

Critics and tech bloggers haven't minced their words in voicing their criticism over BeyondYou's decision to bring his son, an outsider, to lead the exemplary culture that—until now—has been guarded zealously by its late founder. "The apprehension is not unfounded. By all measures, Daniel Reed, Jr., seems to share only one thing in common with his father: his name," an anonymous source said. "Reed's recent press conference fiasco [when he walked off stage after his teleprompter malfunctioned] might be a red and very large warning flag."

Whether Mr. Daniel Reed, Jr., lacks the Reed communication rudder needed to steady BeyondYou's ship is yet to be seen, probably much sooner than later.

"You want it back?" Chris smiled as she offered the article.

"Toss it." Daniel adjusted his tie. "I've memorized it." He smiled.

"Looks like the board members are waiting for you. Are you ready?"

"Do I look like I'm ready?" Daniel forced himself to stop pacing the corner of her office like a boxer in the corner of the ring, ready to face his opponent.

Breathe. Don't pass out! You are Daniel Reed. You can do this. "Is the air conditioning back on yet?" He loosened his tie. "I'm dying here."

"You may want to put this on." She handed him the navy blue jacket he'd draped over the leather chair near the office door. Seconds later they were in the hallway headed toward the elevator.

Daniel tugged at his neck. "I'm dying of heat, and I'm about to tear off this tie."

"Yeah, I think everyone's going to know that." Chris pointed to the enormous sweat stains under his arms as she pressed the button for the lobby. "Sorry. I'm going to run and get an extra floor fan. Who knows when the air conditioning may come back on and how hot that conference room is already."

"Just great." Daniel followed her into the elevator and forced himself to put on the jacket. "That's just what I need—cranky and sweaty executives. Fifteen minutes will probably be all they need to vote me out and run for the pool."

Ten seconds later the elevator door slid open and Chris dashed out. "Think cool thoughts, Daniel. I'll meet you in five minutes tops. Start without me if you have to. You know what you need to say."

The door closed behind her, and Daniel chided himself for not running after her and offering to help carry the fan. Then suddenly, he felt a jolt in the gut.

For a second, he saw himself abandoned at the curb on his first day of school as his mother drove off. Then the truth hit. The elevator had stopped working. Darkness, followed by floodlights, confirmed the reality that faced him.

"You've got to be kidding!" he spoke into the darkness.

"Hello, this is Larry, head of security." A voice from the elevator loudspeaker startled him. "Is anyone stuck in there?"

"Yes, yes." Daniel tried to look around, but all he could see was inky darkness. The stifling black and still, damp air was disorienting. "This is Daniel Reed." As he spoke his name, a sense of calm quietly spread over him.

"Ok. Don't worry, Mr. Reed. We're working on restoring the power and should get you out of there very soon."

Daniel slid to the floor and rested his head against the wall. "I'm not going anywhere," he whispered to no one. He loosened his tie and wiped away the sweat running down his face. His shirt was soaked. He thought of taking it off but couldn't muster the energy.

The irony of the moment struck, and he began laughing, at first a quiet chuckle, then the emotion rising until his shoulders shook. A few days ago, he'd walked out of the same elevator, kicking and screaming, dreading his meeting with the mysterious Bridge Builder. Now, here he was alone in the dark with only himself.

Helpless. At the end of himself. Alone.

Wondering whether all he'd learned would be enough to face the men and women of BeyondYou's board—the people who would perhaps be his executioners.

And realizing for the first time that helpless and alone may be the best place to be when the time has come to stop fighting and begin building.

 **Bridge Builder Notes**

Critics are all around us. They live to predict our success or failure based on our past performance. Sometimes, the greatest critic you'll face is yourself.

- What critics are you facing right now?
- Have they succeeded finding residence in your daily thoughts?
- How are they sabotaging your resolve to move forward?

CHAPTER 3

DOUBT

Monday morning, Daniel stepped into the sleek glass elevator that would take him to his scheduled appointment with the Bridge Builder. He fought the urge to push the button that would return him to the basement parking lot and free him from all this nonsense. A voice inside him told him to wait, and seconds later he stepped out into the bright, modern lobby of MonikerTech. He paused for a moment, taking in the impressive view of the San Diego Bay and Coronado Bay Bridge reflected through the floor-to-ceiling windows. The view was inspiring but incidental. He was about to meet the Bridge Builder.

What in the world am I doing here?

Daniel rolled his neck to work out the knot that tightened into a fist between his shoulders when he felt stressed. His flight from San Francisco to San Diego had been short, giving him little time to think about the mysterious person his father had referred to as the Bridge Builder. He'd spent most of the flight reading blog comments and tweets about the press conference fiasco. If that wasn't enough, back at home, Lynda had punctuated their last fight with a text message: "Daniel, I love you, but you shut me out before a conversation begins. Years ago you won my love because you spoke straight to my heart. *That* Daniel seldom speaks to me any more. I'm praying he's the man who returns to our marriage."

I can't deal with this right now.

Daniel turned off his phone and slammed it down on the table in front of him. What on earth was she talking about? He'd won the woman of his dreams. He'd achieved success in business far beyond most men he knew.

He was in uncharted territory, and he didn't like it. Lack of confidence had never been a problem for him—at least until now. He'd graduated at the top of his class from one of the most prestigious business schools in the country. Being recruited as CFO by a hot startup had boosted his self-confidence. Persuading a woman like Lynda to marry him made him feel invincible. But suddenly it seemed as if everyone was measuring him on the basis of his weaknesses.

He'd never expected life to go off the tracks this way. Even Lynda doubted him now. His throat constricted, and the muscles in his chest slowly began to tighten. He sucked in a gulp of air as he tried to divert his thoughts and refocus on the business of BeyondYou. He couldn't shake the thought that the board's choice of a second Daniel Reed to stand at the helm of BeyondYou had been nothing more than a sleight-of-hand move to inspire confidence among investors, not a vote of confidence in his ability to lead the company.

For the first time in his life, Daniel felt like an impostor. But even worse, for the first time in his life, he feared he was disappointing Lynda.

He knew deep inside he'd not inherited his father's eloquence and ability to persuade gatekeepers, employees, and investors. Even his father's greatest critics had eventually come around and become his most vocal fans and allies. *"How did he do that?"* Daniel had often wondered, but he'd been too proud to seek his father's advice or to admit he needed it.

But his father's letter had finally provided the clue he'd been waiting for. He could only hope that in the next week, the Bridge Builder could deliver something of value—a strategy. He needed something tangible he could take home to the board, to BeyondYou, but most of all to the woman he loved.

Still, Daniel was apprehensive. Why did the meeting have to take place on the campus of MonikerTech, the young but wealthy semiconductor company, led by none other than rock star Michael Thompson—whose legendary accomplishments were recognized world-wide? Michael had every reason to see BeyondYou as ripe for the picking.

Well, here we go, Daniel thought as he approached the reception counter.

"Good morning. You must be Mr. Reed." The receptionist's greeting was warm and professional as she stood and extended her hand to Daniel. "I'm Becky." Her dimpled smile reminded him of Lynda.

"And I'm Daniel Reed."

"You're all checked in. I called the Bridge Builder as soon as I saw you." Becky handed him a security badge with his name and picture. "She's on her way down to meet you."

"*She?* I mean she goes by Bridge Builder?" Daniel tried to conceal his surprise and his lack of preparation for this meeting. *Why hadn't Paul told him that the Bridge Builder was a woman?* He scolded himself and observed that it was becoming a habit.

"Yes, everyone calls her Bridge Builder around here. You'll get used to it," Becky reassured him.

The fact that this Bridge Builder was a woman wasn't the issue—half of his board members and executives were women. Plus, Lynda brought home twice his salary through media endorsements alone. But the fact that he'd assumed the Bridge Builder was a man highlighted how unprepared he was for their meeting, not to mention how disconnected he'd been from his father.

Daniel thanked Becky, walked over to the window, and stared at the water of the San Diego Bay sparkling in the distance. Taking a deep breath, he applied pressure to his temples, something he'd learned in grad school when he felt a tension headache coming on. He was beginning to feel the weight of the pressure to do this thing right, whatever that meant. And it certainly didn't help that this meeting was taking place so soon after his father's death, even before he had the opportunity to meet with the entire board.

Once again, he tried to quiet the voices of the analysts and the media jabbering in his head—the constant background chatter, the audience waiting to confirm that Daniel Reed, Jr., would never be The Great Daniel Reed.

Maybe they're right.

The anxious thought had crossed Daniel's mind hundreds of times. In fact, staring at the San Diego Bay, Daniel felt like a child who'd been given a monumental homework assignment—first from his father and then from Paul. And now—and perhaps most importantly—from Lynda.

His thoughts were interrupted by the sound of the elevator door opening behind him. His life was about to change, and he had no idea how. His father's gift felt like a shove through a door that would lead to his future.

He just couldn't decide if it was a door he wanted to walk through.

 **Bridge Builder Notes**

Doubts are fear—and the greatest barrier you'll face when you decide to go for something bigger, something you've always wanted. Fear about your competence, credibility, timing, or return on investment can put a halt on your progress.

- What doubts, attitudes, or habits are keeping you from moving forward toward your goal?

- Which ones are legitimate obstacles?
- Which ones do you think could be more easily overcome if you had the right tools?

CHAPTER 4

OPPORTUNITY

H i, Daniel. Chris Mason. It's so nice to finally meet you in person." The Bridge Builder offered a firm yet friendly handshake. "I'm so glad you decided to come early," she continued without missing a beat. "I hope you're hungry. I thought it would be nice to get acquainted over breakfast. MonikerTech's chef makes a mean omelet."

Well it's good to know that this Bridge Builder has a real name. Daniel followed the affable brunette across the lobby and on to the outdoor courtyard.

"Made-to-order omelets with the San Diego Bay as our backdrop— this is as good as it gets, isn't it?"

"Ms. Mason . . ." Daniel tried but failed to conceal his impatience. Chatting over omelets and San Diego's blue skies wasn't really at the top of his list of priorities. "Can we get this show on the road?"

The Bridge Builder responded with a wry smile. "You remind me of your father. Do you know that those were the exact words he said to me on our first formal meeting?"

Daniel stopped in the middle of the courtyard and turned toward her. "Why am I really here, Ms. Mason?" He struggled to assume the most polite tone he could muster. "And why should I take an entire week to listen to you when I should be preparing to lead BeyondYou?" he continued before she had the opportunity to answer.

"You can call me Chris," she said as she continued her trek toward the omelet station and pulled a plate from the service line. "You read my mind, Daniel. I actually had planned to ask you the same thing. Why are you here?"

Daniel wasn't used to searching for words. He didn't like feeling out of control or like he was a pawn on someone else's chessboard. But Chris Mason clearly wasn't stopping and waiting for a response. She'd already made her breakfast selections and was headed toward the tables.

And she clearly expected him to follow.

 **Bridge Builder Notes**

Opportunity often is disguised in unlikely mentors—those who have traveled where you want to go and are willing to tell you how to get there.

- What opportunities are opening before you in the form of mentors and personal connections?
- How prepared are you to follow and make the most of the time you have with them?

CHAPTER 5

DOUBLESPEAK

My father forced me to come."

The words were ready to spill from Daniel's lips when he heard Michael Thompson's unmistakable baritone echo across the courtyard.

"Good morning, Bridge Builder. Wait till you try our Chef's Monday Surprise. Not what you'd expect for breakfast. I'll tell you one thing—they ain't your momma's Brussels sprouts!"

"Good morning, Michael," answered Chris as he approached the square table she'd chosen near the fountain. He sat beside her and across from the chair Daniel had chosen after rushing through the line. "Let me introduce you to . . ."

"Daniel Reed!" Michael interrupted, extending his hand in what seemed like a genuinely affectionate gesture. "I think the entire world knows your face, Son. My deepest and most sincere condolences regarding your father's untimely passing. A great loss to the world indeed. He had a tremendous influence on my life—as I'm sure on many others, too."

Daniel tossed his head. *Who are you calling "Son"? If you think I'm going to let you intimidate me, you have no idea who you're dealing with, Mr. Michael Thompson.* That's what Daniel wanted to say. Instead he managed to mumble, "Thank you for your hospitality, Mr. Thompson. I appreciate you allowing me to steal Chris this week."

"Daniel just arrived, Michael. He hasn't seen the Blueprint yet," interjected Chris to clarify Daniel's comment. "You won't be stealing only *me*, Daniel. Michael insisted on having a meeting slot at the end of your stay."

"Blueprint?"

"The plan, the roadmap. You know—an agenda of sorts," clarified Chris.

Daniel could feel his tension headache returning. *Oh, boy, I can smell an ambush. Then again, what if there is something more to the gift? What if this is a sinister test devised by BeyondYou's board? Or maybe my father has left me an opportunity to leverage my proximity with Michael Thompson.*

"Can't wait," answered Michael as he stood up, interrupting Daniel's thoughts. "By the way, call me Michael—and don't forget to grab some of those Brussels sprouts," he said as he walked off and headed for the atrium across the courtyard.

One thing Daniel knew for sure—whether the Blueprint outlined a test, an ambush, or an opportunity, he would need to play his cards just right to find out.

 **Bridge Builder Notes**

Imagine that your thoughts were displayed across your forehead like subtitles in a foreign movie. Would they match the words you are speaking? Doublespeak, the type of language that deliberately disguises, distorts, or conceals the truth, is the fastest way to burn bridges before they're built.

- How much of the time do you engage in doublespeak?
- In what ways has doublespeak affected your ability to genuinely connect with someone else?

CHAPTER 6

COMMON GROUND

D aniel's eyes followed Michael, who stopped to shake the hands of employees eating under the black and white striped table umbrellas. Daniel shook his head, thinking how long it took Michael to cross the courtyard before disappearing behind the glass doors of the massive atrium.

"Can I ask a question?" asked Daniel, eager to change gears and finally satisfy his nagging curiosity. "What's behind the name?—Bridge Builder, I mean." He hated feeling like he might be the only person in the business world who didn't know why Chris was known by such a unique identity.

"Ah, yes," Chris smiled. "Your father never told you the story?"

"Maybe he did—or tried," Daniel replied, surprised by the candor that had crept into his voice.

"Yes, I imagine it might be hard to listen to your father when he's the mighty Daniel Reed," she smiled warmly. "I lost my dad when I was a child, so I'd like to think that I would have listened to anything he would've had to say. Of course, hindsight is always 20/20, right?"

"I'm learning that." A moment of silence followed as they looked at each other, forks in hand, challenging the other to be the first to try one of the highly praised Brussels sprouts. Daniel made the first move and dove in, and Chris followed and scooped a mound onto her plate.

In a moment they were both nodding with delight and approval, allowing themselves to enjoy the moment.

Daniel couldn't ignore the calming effect Chris had on him. He was in unchartered territory. He wasn't used to connecting with someone in such a short period of time. But something about this mysterious Bridge Builder was disarming. She couldn't be much older than fifty, but her bright brown eyes and joyful smile made her seem fresh and youthful. In some ways, she reminded him of his late mother—and Lynda, his wife. Chris carried herself with the same unceremonious transparency and unassuming confidence that inspired trust.

"So what's behind my name?" Chris echoed Daniel's question, breaking the silence. "Well, I can tell you that I have your father to thank for the moniker, no pun intended.

"I met Daniel about twenty-five years ago at a startup incubator event. I was speaking on how to build bridges to the hearts and minds of investors. He had lost three different bids for angel funding and was getting ready to pitch to a venture capital group. He hired me to help him craft a compelling story and fine-tune his pitch. Shortly after, BeyondYou had the funding it needed; and the rest is history."

If there was one thing Daniel knew he could use at this point in his life, it was the knowledge of how to build bridges to the hearts and minds of his audiences—and first on that list included the Board of Directors he had yet to meet. "It's hard to remember a time when my father wasn't the consummate communicator. Well, except when . . ."

"Except when he swore?"

"You knew that?"

"Oh yes. But you know who cured him of that, don't you?"

"Yes, Mom." Daniel chuckled. It was nice to discover common ground. "He used to drive her crazy. When he was upset, he'd just let the expletives fly, but she wouldn't put up with it. 'Dirty mouths are not allowed in this house,' she used to say." They laughed.

"The day she died, my father and I promised to honor her memory by abstaining from cussing from that day on. He kept his promise—and I nearly got my mouth washed with soap when I forgot."

"Great story. Your mom was a remarkable woman, one of the greatest Bridge Builders I've ever known."

Daniel got up from his chair and cleared his throat. He picked up the dirty plates from the table and walked to the busboy station nearby. When he returned to the table, he'd composed his voice once again. He'd come to meet this woman for a reason. It was time to get this show on the road.

 **Bridge Builder Notes**

Finding common ground with others is a gift and can be an unexpected opportunity. It happens when we're willing to put aside our personal agenda.

- When was the last time you put your agenda aside to find common ground with someone else?
- How would your communication change if your goal were to find common ground with others?

CHAPTER 7

TUG OF WAR

aniel followed Chris across the courtyard and through the glass doors of the three-story atrium in the middle of the campus. Her sleek but comfortable office was on the third floor. Floor-to-ceiling windows overlooked the bay. As Daniel followed Chris through the doors of her office, he wondered if she could sense his anxious energy. His mind raced as he took in the view of the MonikerTech campus. He remembered seeing pictures of the conceptual design featured in *Forbes* a while back and making a mental note to read the article. He never did.

"Make yourself comfortable, Daniel." Chris closed the door behind her and led him to the cozy sitting area, where four teal leather chairs surrounded a glass coffee table.

Daniel couldn't help but think about "The Blueprint." Looking back, it seemed as if Chris and Michael had been talking about a secret strategy, and he was the target, a thought that raised his body temperature.

"Daniel, I know you are probably eager to get started. And I'm sure you have a lot of questions."

"Actually, Chris, I'm grateful for this opportunity. Giving me a week is extremely generous of you. The board only gave me three days." He gave up trying to sound witty.

Chris sat back and relaxed comfortably in the chair across from Daniel. He could tell that she was anticipating his objection. She remained silent, and he took the opportunity to get a few things off his chest.

"As I said in my email," Daniel continued, "I only have one question, or one focus, rather, for our conversation: *How can I be more persuasive?*" He emphasized the phrase for effect. "Frankly, Chris, I don't think our conversation warrants five days." Daniel shifted to the edge of his seat and leaned forward. He felt the surge of energy rising. It was time he started acting like the CEO of BeyondYou, not like the "Son" Michael had addressed in the courtyard. If he was going to prove to the board that he could lead BeyondYou, he'd better start now.

"Chris," Daniel continued, barely taking a breath, "I need to get back to BeyondYou and prepare for a series of presentations and meetings. And I'm sure you have work to do here as well. Do you understand what I'm saying?"

"Daniel, I understand perfectly. You value brevity."

"Yes!" Daniel realized his response was more euphoric than a dignified CEO's should probably be. Still, he was pleased his point had been made.

"I value brevity, too." She paused. "I do realize that a week here may seem like overkill, Daniel . . ."

He cut her off. "It is, Chris. It really is." Daniel just needed the formula. *Tell me what to do next, and I'll be out of your hair.* She needed to understand that he wasn't the type who got all gushy about professional development retreats. In fact, he despised them.

"Daniel, the Blueprint I've prepared . . ."

He interrupted again. "It can be modified, I'm sure." This was a tug of war he needed to win. His father had succeeded in putting him in this time-wasting position, but he was not going to dictate from the grave how long Daniel would have to endure it. He had an Ivy League education, for goodness sake. He had managed to land a pretty enviable CFO job without participating in touchy-feely training and coaching sessions. And he had managed to snag Lynda Briggs from Mr. Fancy Pants Lawyer, her former fiancé! And he wasn't about to let people forget that BeyondYou had come knocking at his door before his father's body had been placed in the grave!

Chris paused and took a sip of water. She didn't seem affected in the least.

"Yes, Daniel. The Blueprint can be modified if that's what you really want. But my preparation for these meetings was based on *your* request."

"Excuse me?"

"If I remember the words of your last email correctly—and do correct me if I'm wrong—you said, 'My father gave you a great deal of credit for his success. I would like to *learn exactly*,'" she emphasized the last two words, "'how you were able to do that.' Do I remember your request correctly?"

Daniel knew he had lost, long before they had begun. "Yes. That's what I said."

Chris sat back in her chair without changing her tone or facial expression.

Daniel struggled to mask the frustration and anger washing over him. He needed to get back to work and prove to the board he was the leader they needed. He didn't need five days of sensitivity training, or even worse, someone pointing out how he'd failed to turn out like his father.

He needed to get out of this place as fast as possible. And he was going to make sure he got what he wanted. And just like that—when he thought he was about to lose his grip—Chris offered him a way out, followed by a flash of memory: the words of Lynda's final email reminding him that BeyondYou was no longer his first or greatest priority.

Bridge Builder Notes

Tugs of war. Struggles. Resistance. With ourselves or others, we face them at every turn. Some are worth the fight. Some are worth letting go.

- What battles are you engaged in—with yourself or with others?
- Is resistance worth the potential end result?
- What will you gain if you decide to stop resisting?

CHAPTER 8

SURRENDER

I s that still what you want?" Chris asked.

Chris's words jarred him back into the moment.

"Is that still what you want? To learn how to be successful? To learn principles that will make you a better leader and communicator? To learn from another successful leader what perhaps you have not yet mastered yourself, in order to grow? Are you open to the idea of learning, Daniel? Gaining new skills that will help you connect with the people who are at the core of your life, your vision, your dreams?"

He felt the fight drain from him as pictures of Lynda's tear-streaked face flashed through his mind. And BeyondYou? Was he *really* ready for the challenge?

Daniel sat in silence for what seemed like an eternity. Chris seemed to be genuine, free of manipulation. He relaxed in his chair and looked out the window, fixing his eyes on the Coronado Bridge. Her gentle questions had opened a fresh wound, as well as old ones—and he felt more vulnerable than he'd allowed himself to be for a long time.

"I wonder how many times my father wished he could have shared his wisdom with me. I refused to listen, Chris. I was stubborn and angry and stupid. It seems silly, doesn't it? How many people would have paid to learn from the great Daniel Reed? I didn't value his knowledge, track record, or experience . . ." That's what Daniel wanted to say, but being sentimental wasn't his style. Instead, he allowed the silence to linger as the tension for a response grew.

Every passing minute made it increasingly clear that Chris would let the silence remain until he answered her question. Her maternal smile lightened the air, making it easier than he thought to breathe deeply and surrender—at least for this battle.

"Yes. I still want that," Daniel finally answered. The words were more than words. He did want to learn. For a moment he allowed himself to wonder where that journey would take him.

Bridge Builder Notes

Surrender costs us something—often it's mere pride. Whether letting go is worth the cost, only you can decide.

- What is the cost of surrendering a fight you've been holding onto for some time?
- What will you lose and what will you gain if you surrender?
- Is the cost worth it?

CHAPTER 9

THE ARMOR

C hris had quietly observed Daniel's familiar hesitation—a hesitation she knew well. She'd detected the same hesitation years earlier when she first met the late Daniel Reed, and then when she met Michael Thompson. In fact, she was used to dealing with the type of armor many high achievers feel they need to wear to convey confidence while concealing their insecurities.

Penetrating that armor was part of her signature brand of coaching leaders in how to grow and developing Bridge Builders. She knew that people who excel at the highest levels of leadership and influence find it difficult to be vulnerable and admit they need help getting something they really want.

Daniel, like his father, would have to come to that realization on his own. But unfortunately, Daniel didn't have the luxury of time. Chris suspected that in just a few days, he would be competing against the clock—and the countdown would start the moment he stepped in front of the BeyondYou board.

For now, Chris would just have to trust the process and let Daniel come around on his own time. "I'm glad we're on the same page, Daniel," she responded, as she reached for a leather portfolio and handed it to him. "A gift."

Daniel ran his fingers over the embossing. *"Everything is part of the lesson,"* he read aloud. "It's exquisite. Thank you."

Chris had planned to discuss the Blueprint with Daniel during this early session, but his guardedness meant it would be more important to take other steps first. She could already see Daniel's tendency to get caught up in the details, and right now he needed to get a vision for the bigger picture. So instead, she gave him instructions to take an electronic assessment she planned to discuss with him later in the week. Daniel's armor would first have to come off before she could make an impact.

For now, she'd succeeded in making a vital connection with Daniel's heart. He wasn't quite ready to move closer and trust her, but they still had time. Her first priority was to make a connection with the things that were occupying his mind—his questionable ability to lead BeyondYou successfully. Chris knew exactly whose help she needed to enlist as she helped Daniel assess his leadership abilities.

By the end of the day, she would know if this budding CEO would have a fighting chance at BeyondYou.

 **Bridge Builder Notes**

Armor, as a useful apparatus, shields and protects you from harm. As a barrier, it keeps others from accessing you and connecting with you.

- When are you most likely to wear the type of armor Chris describes?
- How is it preventing you from connecting with others and what you want?

CHAPTER 10

ASSUMPTIONS VS. INTENTIONS

D aniel spotted a poster as he walked beside Chris across the atrium to their next meeting. The content immediately captured his interest: an upcoming Bridge Builder Leadership Symposium. His mind began to form a list of questions when he caught sight of Michael Thompson walking toward them, busily absorbed by his smart phone. Daniel sent up a silent prayer that Michael would keep his head down and miss them, since the last thing Daniel needed right now was another Michael Thompson encounter.

But no such luck. Michael had spotted them, slipped his phone in his pocket, and immediately headed their way.

Daniel took a deep breath and straightened his back, rallying all the executive presence he could muster as he greeted Michael.

"You aren't tweeting about me are you?" Daniel tried to keep his tone light, but was mortified to hear the arrogance in his tone. Michael was known to be a Twitter ninja in the business world, and every time Daniel had seen his fingers hover over his phone, he'd broken into a sweat. The man had over four hundred thousand Twitter followers, and thousands of readers followed his blog.

"I've thought about it," answered Michael with a playful smirk, "but it's probably not a good idea, right, Bridge Builder?"

Daniel jumped in before she could answer. "I'd be careful with the tweets, unless you want the wrong story to go viral." Too late Daniel realized that his choice of words might have insulted his host. Yet, it wasn't a secret that business analysts had speculated for years about "the perfect merger" between BeyondYou and MonikerTech. They predicted that a merger would birth a Goliath that could dominate several niches in the tech industry. Without his father at the helm, BeyondYou's vulnerability was all the buzz. Daniel knew everyone expected to see how he would maneuver the rumors, which were already running high, suggesting that MonikerTech finally had the advantage it needed to go after BeyondYou.

Michael crossed his arms. "So have you got any tweet ideas for me, Son?" Michael's serious tone startled Daniel. He couldn't tell if Michael was offended or if he was trying to intimidate him.

"A good piece of communication advice, perhaps?" Daniel silently congratulated himself for his quick recovery.

Michael smiled. "Good one!" He dropped his head for a moment as his fingers flew across the keypad of his phone. When he was done, he gave Chris a smile and Daniel a pat on the shoulder. "Enjoy the journey, Son. See you on Friday." Then he headed down a polished granite hallway and slipped into an elevator.

Daniel pulled out his phone to see what Michael had tweeted as he disappeared behind the elevator doors. He read the words and swallowed.

"What communication wisdom did Michael share with the world?" Chris asked.

"My wife would have loved to see this," Daniel said. "Assume positive intentions or build a bridge to nowhere. #Communication #Advice" He turned his phone to show Chris the tweet.

"And why is that?"

He paused. "Well, she tells me I can act like a jerk and speak without thinking, and I need to be put in my place from time to time. But Lynda would say it more kindly than that. She's always reminding me that I only hurt myself when I think everyone's out to get me."

"I like her already." Chris smiled.

The concern and hurt in his wife's face flashed before Daniel's eyes as he remembered the talk they'd had before he'd left on the trip. He hadn't listened, and she'd shut down. He swallowed as he remembered the words of her email. And the words in Michael's tweet rebuked him.

Or build a bridge to nowhere . . .

Michael's words replayed like a broken record as Daniel continued down hallways and through conference areas with Chris. A vision of the board and the men and women he would face at the upcoming meeting haunted him—his toughest audience ever.

The choice would be his. To return the same man he had been when he left. Or to build a bridge to a new, brighter future for BeyondYou.

And for Lynda.

His true obstacle was slowly becoming clear. The one thing that threatened his future was his pride.

 **Bridge Builder Notes**

Assume positive intentions. Easier said than done.

- Assuming negative or positive intentions—what comes easier for you?
- How can Michael's simple advice improve the quality of your personal and professional relationships?

CHAPTER 11

EVIDENCE

D aniel, let me introduce you to Tammy Parker, MonikerTech's Chief Sustainability Officer," said Chris when they arrived at her office.

"I'm surprised to hear that MonikerTech has a Chief Sustainability Officer." Daniel sat directly across from Tammy at the small conference table, wondering what was in the large, red binder beside her. "I can't wait to hear why I'm meeting with one." Daniel silently cringed as he spoke. There it was again, the cynical edge in his voice that usually got him in trouble.

Tammy seemed unaffected. "Yes, I can see why you would be surprised. The role of sustainability officer at MonikerTech is unique," she said as she settled in her black leather chair. "In addition to leading green initiatives, I also lead sustainability as it relates to our corporate culture, namely the Bridge Builder Leadership Initiative that the Bridge Builder is helping us implement."

"Okay. You have my full attention." Daniel opened his notebook and uncapped his pen, feeling annoyed that he'd forgotten his tablet at home. He tried to put it out of his mind. Perhaps this meeting would finally give him the substance he was looking for, the conversation about strategy he'd wanted to have from the very beginning. He still couldn't understand why Michael was letting him see under MonikerTech's hood, but that was a question for another day. "What do you mean by Bridge Builder Leadership?"

Chris smiled and sat back, letting Tammy carry the conversation. "Bridge Builder Leadership is the collective name we use to describe our strategic approach to onboarding new employees and systematically developing our human capital. We believe in growing a culture of Bridge Builders."

"And by Bridge Builders, you mean . . ." Daniel was poised, pen in hand, like a litigator conducting a deposition.

"What do you think it means?"

Daniel didn't bother to hide his annoyance. He was here to get answers, and beating around the bush was wasting precious time. Strangely, his mother's words rushed to mind. *Remember your manners when you're someone's guest.* He put his pen down and sat back in his chair. "I imagine you're talking about people who know how to build relationships. But I'm more interested in hearing exactly what that means."

"You're right," Tammy responded. "More specifically, Bridge Builders are individuals who seek to reach the hearts and minds of their audiences by choosing to communicate differently, intentionally using a specific set of principles."

Reach the hearts and minds of audiences—the same words his father had written in his letter and the key point of contention between them. Daniel took a deep breath and fought to quiet the wave of emotion that had struck. *All this touchy-feely mumbo-jumbo is a distraction from business strategy, metrics, and data-driven decision-making.* He let the words go and decided to ask for proof instead.

"To what end?"

"To build relationships. To facilitate productive dialogue. To improve collaboration."

Daniel laid his pen down. "Are you saying that MonikerTech's culture is all about communication development?"

"Yes—and no. We believe communication development is leadership development, and thus the single-most important investment we make in our employees. Frankly, it's the most valuable investment companies can make in their success."

"Communication development? Really?" Daniel couldn't hide his surprise. He picked up his pen.

Tammy continued. "If you think about it, every aspect of a company's success hinges on successful communication. From pitching to investors, to negotiation, to sales and marketing, to running meetings that lead to innovation and productivity, to teamwork and collaboration, to technical staff being able to communicate ideas effectively to non-technical constituents—not to mention the crucial role of communication in customer service and global strategic partnerships."

Daniel's mind was racing. He wasn't convinced yet, but she was hitting a chord. Once again, Tammy was echoing words he had heard his late father preach. Daniel had fought them more than once. He'd argued that a numbers guy who wrote code as a hobby, for example, didn't need to make communication development his top priority.

Tammy interrupted his thoughts. "Do you know that most companies spend less than 1 percent of their operating budget on developing their employees?" Her passion for the subject was evident. "And when they do invest in staff development, the investment is random and sporadic—not strategic, ongoing, and focused on giving employees the communication tools that can transform the culture, ensure employees' personal and professional success—and increase *the bottom line of the business.*"

Daniel's ears perked up. He wasn't fully convinced yet. In his previous role as Chief Financial Officer, his primary focus had been to keep spending in check. Training and development expenses, in his mind, were luxuries, not necessities. For instance, when he approved funding for a leadership retreat, he felt like he was flushing money down the toilet. He could never see how the expense affected the bottom line of the business.

He wasn't about to admit it, but he also had personal issues with the whole notion of communication. The words he had loathed for the last two days came to mind: "Daniel Reed may lack the communication rudder needed to steady BeyondYou's ship." What he hated most about the words is that they were true. Creating presentations and leading effective meetings were his Achilles' heel. He'd resigned himself to the fact that he was the numbers guy, the Excel guy, and the money guy— because he hadn't inherited his father's charisma, eloquence, and gift of persuasion.

And how could he forget his communication issues at home? More than once Lynda said that communication—or the lack thereof—was the root of all their challenges.

And now? For the first time in their marriage, he seemed to be losing her trust. If he ever needed to understand the emotion behind her words—what she truly needed—it was now.

Tammy interrupted his reverie. "Communication costs business more than we're willing to admit. We know without a shadow of a doubt that our competitors are lagging because they're absorbing well over twenty-five thousand dollars a year—per employee—for internal communication challenges . . ." Clearly, Tammy had found a direct path to Daniel's shortcomings and was laying down her arguments, patiently and methodically.

"These communication challenges directly affect H.R. Downtime, safety, retention, turnover, productivity, and performance."

Daniel didn't need to write anything down. As a former CFO, he daily contended with the costs associated with the factors Tammy just mentioned. He had held meeting after meeting, trying to find a way to lower these costs. Never once did he connect them to communication.

"Safety costs alone can bankrupt a company," she continued. What good is it to have safety signage all over the place if the corporate culture minimizes the importance of communication?" Daniel remained silent.

"And don't even get me started with the costs associated with change—which is the only constant we'll ever have in our industry. Survey after survey confirms that two thirds of employees don't receive enough useful information during corporate change. Customer surveys are not much different."

She paused and slid the red binder in front of him. "The data is all here, Daniel."

He flipped opened the binder. Three tabs divided a thick stack of paper—Surveys, Case Studies, Raw Data. "Can I borrow it?"

"Keep it." She smiled. "I'm already convinced. But I'd suggest you get a cup of coffee before you settle in to read it."

"I'm pretty sure it's going to take a pot or two," Daniel spoke under his breath as he closed the binder and tucked it into his briefcase.

 **Bridge Builder Notes**

Evidence about the impact of poor communication in the workplace abounds, but not everyone is paying attention.

- Where is communication most effective in your workplace?
- Where is communication jeopardizing results in your workplace?

CHAPTER 12

LAST-DITCH EFFORT

Not every brilliant employee can or should be expected to be a great communicator, right?" Daniel's voice matched Tammy's passion. "I mean, can we really expect that everyone can become a Bridge Builder?" *And aren't some people like me destined to be handicapped communicators for life?* It still wasn't safe enough to say the words out loud. He spoke as he stirred cream into a yellow ceramic mug of coffee from a display of beverages at the kitchenette at the end of the room.

"The Bridge Builder assures us that everyone innately knows how to be one—but people don't remember, nor do they choose to think, act, or communicate like one."

Out of the corner of his eye, Daniel caught Chris's smile.

"If she's wrong, we're paying her too much money."

"Really?" Daniel ignored Tammy's second comment as he walked back to the conference table.

"The bottom line, Daniel, is that anyone who *wants* to become a Bridge Builder can become one. It's a matter of intention—not perfection. It's a choice. That's what being a Bridge Builder is all about."

Daniel hesitated for a moment, but he wasn't ready to give up. "Let's say that the next up-and-coming tech god is trying to decide whether to come and work for MonikerTech or for one of the other ten companies that are courting him." He smirked.

"Okay, let's," Tammy smiled back.

"Let's assume he likes the laidback San Diego culture, so MonikerTech is looking pretty good. Are you picturing this?"

Chris chuckled from her side of the table.

"Okay. I'm picturing it," Tammy said.

"She walks up to Michael Thompson . . ."

Tammy looked at Chris, struggling to contain herself. "Okay, so she's a tech goddess, then."

"Whatever. He/she tells Michael, 'I'm here to make you a LOT of money, not to communicate. Communication isn't my forte, and it will never be. Take it or leave it.'"

Tammy composed herself and assumed her professional tone. "That would be a sad day indeed. Talent without the willingness to consider the benefits of bridge building reveals a rigidity, which likely affects other areas beyond communication."

Daniel was silent. He didn't want to re-live any of the conversations with his father that had begun on the topic of close-mindedness and ended with a fight. For that matter, he didn't want to think about any similar conversation-fights with Lynda either.

"Michael would be the first one to say it," Tammy continued. "You can ask him yourself. And if I'm wrong—I'll eat your red binder."

Daniel was silent. He searched for a comeback, but had nothing.

The room was silent for a moment, and then Tammy spoke. "As the Bridge Builder likes to say, 'If you argue for your limitations, you get to keep them.'" She paused. "But never while you're working at MonikerTech."

Bridge Builder Notes

We tend to fight for what we believe to be true or fair—until we are rendered speechless by the realization that we may have been wrong.

- The Bridge Builder says, "Everyone innately knows how to be a Bridge Builder." Can you remember a time when you built a bridge to someone's heart or mind?
- Tammy says, "If you argue for your limitations, you get to keep them." How does this statement apply to you?

CHAPTER 13

BRIDGE BUILDERS WANTED

A s if on cue, a knock came at the door. A young man wearing a chef's uniform stuck his head in the room, announcing that he was delivering a morning snack, courtesy of Michael Thompson. Never had a break for brain food sounded so good to Daniel. He followed Chris and Tammy to the sumptuous mini buffet that the jovial young man set up at a table near the kitchenette. Daniel filled a small plate as his father's words echoed in his mind. *Son, if you argue for your limitations, you get to keep them.* The same words Tammy had spoken to him.

Obviously, his father had listened and learned. The sentence had become his mantra. But was it possible that all these years Daniel had been the cause of his own limitations?

"Looks like you have a lot on your mind," Tammy said as she followed Daniel back to the table. "We can take a break if you'd like some time to think about a few things." She pulled out her chair and sat as Daniel chose a chair across the table.

"No, I'm fine. The conversation just takes me back to talks I've had before."

"Of course." Tammy sipped a glass of orange juice. "I'm sure you have a lot to think about. It's always sad for me when I meet talented individuals—those who have the potential to do great work for the company, to become great leaders with greater influence, who argue and fight for their right to remain ordinary or mediocre communicators."

Daniel ignored the innuendo, but he couldn't help but appreciate the passion in her voice.

"Do you encounter many of those kinds of people here at MonikerTech?" he asked.

"Never," Tammy answered.

"Really?" Daniel found it hard to believe. In fact, he didn't want to believe it.

"They'd be a detriment to our culture. My job as Sustainability Officer is to prevent that at all cost."

"You don't think that's a little harsh?" Daniel stabbed a wedge of melon.

"Harsh? I can see you're puzzled. Let me tell you about my first job out of college. I couldn't find a job in my field, so I took a job as a customer service banker. Several times a day I had to interface with CT, the head of new accounts, and the resident communication terrorist. At her worst, she was opinionated, sarcastic, passive-aggressive, and insensitive. At her best, she was indifferent. She made everyone's lives a living hell, especially because so many people needed to interface with her department. Soon, everyone learned to avoid her by developing workarounds. But CT was all anyone could talk about. During breaks. During lunch. During work-related socials. At the copy machine. At the water cooler. Inside the vault. And soon enough conversations trickled into conversations with customers.

"CT was costing the company thousands of dollars in wasted time, employee morale, and unhappy customers who eventually left."

Daniel couldn't help himself. "I think every company has a CT." He rolled his eyes.

"So you've met a CT, too."

"Oh, yeah."

"I hated CT, or so I thought," she continued. "When I left, distance gave me a new perspective. I realized my anger was misdirected.

"CT wasn't the problem. Management was the problem. They chose to keep her and sacrifice the culture."

Tammy reached for her bowl of blueberries as Chris chimed in.

"MonikerTech decided long ago that there's no room here for communicators who hurt the culture—no matter how talented they are. If they don't have the desire to build bridges, they don't belong here."

"Let me see if I understand you correctly," Daniel interrupted. "MonikerTech's hiring objective is to find great communicators?" But before Tammy could respond, he added, "Not managers. Not software engineers. Not designers. Not accountants. You're looking exclusively for . . ."

She cut him off. "Birds of a feather. That's what we want," said Tammy.

"Excuse me?"

"Those who fit our culture of Bridge Builders."

"You may have to let go of a lot of talent then."

"You and I know that the world doesn't have a shortage of talent. We will never experience a shortage of competent candidates for any number of positions. That's the advantage we have. We have the luxury of handpicking the very best employees in their field. We don't simply want talented software engineers. We want team players who've demonstrated they can become Bridge Builders—and who also happen to be talented software engineers or managers or designers or CPAs."

"But didn't you say earlier that everyone already possesses the skills that make Bridge Builders?"

"Yes, but not everyone is intentional about using them. Take you, for example." She smiled, as if clarifying that she had earned the right to push harder. "I don't know you well, Daniel, but I already know you have intentionally used the skills of a Bridge Builder—at least once in your life."

"Really?" Daniel was amused. He chuckled and crossed his arms, daring her to dazzle him with her brilliance. "This ought to be good."

"If my Reed trivia serves me right, you did persuade *the* Lynda Briggs to marry you, did you not?"

Daniel knew that his finest hour had been the day he'd persuaded Lynda that he was the only man for her. He couldn't argue with Tammy.

"Touché. Daniel Reed, Bridge Builder. Who would've thought you'd be right about something so important in my life?"

"Besides," Tammy added, "Communication skills are only part of the equation. The five Bridge Builder Principles keep us from manipulating others for our own selfish gain."

Daniel began to ask about the principles, but decided to postpone that part of the conversation for another day. Tammy had made her point brilliantly, although she wouldn't hear Daniel admit it. Instead, he knew he had to make a phone call he couldn't put off any longer.

It had been too long. A rush of panic raced through his chest, and Daniel suddenly found himself secretly praying that too long didn't really mean too long.

 Bridge Builder Notes

Building a culture of Bridge Builders comes with hard choices not everyone is willing to make.

- Why are "communication terrorists" like CT allowed to remain in the workplace?
- If you could redesign your corporate culture from the ground up, what kind of choices would you make? What kind of people would you bring?

CHAPTER 14

WHAT IF?

D aniel looked at his phone and found a text message from Lynda. The time stamp showed she'd sent it just an hour earlier.

"I love you, Babe. Call me if you want to talk." As always, her timing was impeccable. She seemed to have a sixth sense that nudged her when Daniel needed an extra dose of grace to find his way home after playing the fool.

He excused himself and slipped into the hallway. As the phone rang, he tried to remember why they'd fought before he left home. As usual, he couldn't remember.

"Hi, Babe," she answered. Her voice was warm, and Daniel knew he'd been forgiven before he even spoke. He apologized for being a jerk. The words came from an uncomfortable new awareness of how often his communication hurt her, and he didn't like the feeling.

For the next thirty minutes, he poured out a play-by-play of what he'd experienced so far at MonikerTech. He told her about Chris

Mason, the Bridge Builder. His encounter with Michael Thompson. His suspicions that Michael may want to pounce on BeyondYou. And the highlights of his conversation with Tammy.

"Lynda, I know you've probably been waiting a long time to hear this, but I'm also learning that you've been right all along."

"Tell me more."

"Communication *does* matter—in business and in life. Apparently, I've been too much of an idiot to see that when it doesn't matter, people and businesses and families suffer." He waited for her response, as her silence stretched painfully into what seemed like minutes. Then, finally, the sound of her voice allowed Daniel to breathe again.

"Why are you there this week, Daniel?" Daniel smiled. His wife knew he needed to process obstacles verbally.

"To tell you the truth, I'm not sure. I think my father knew why he sent me here, and the very idea of him sending me off to some kind of remedial business school ticked me off too much to even give it a shot. I'm trying to figure it out as I go. I guess I'm supposed to magically transform into a Bridge Builder slash Superb Communicator who will blow away the hearts and minds of everyone I talk to."

"And your wife's heart, of course."

"Of course."

"Magically, huh? So you're bringing home some pixie dust with you? A secret potion? I like the sound of that!"

"Okay, okay. I get the point." Lynda knew exactly how to usher him out of a pity party. And how to come to his rescue while protecting his dignity.

"Do you trust this Bridge Builder, Daniel? Do you think she can help you?"

"My father trusted her. Michael Thompson apparently does, too."

She cut him off. "Do *you* trust her?"

Daniel took a deep breath. He hadn't wanted to trust her. But everything about her told him that she was genuinely interested in his best interests. "Do you know that she helped my father get funding for BeyondYou?

"No! That can't be right. Mr. Daniel Reed in need of communication skills coaching? Impossible!" Daniel could hear the playfulness in her voice.

"Yes, impossible."

"So—do *you* trust her?" Textbook Lynda. Tenacious. BS intolerant. She let her question hang in the air for what seemed an eternity.

"Yes. I think I trust her."

"Good. So what's the problem, Mr. Reed?"

"I guess there's no problem." She'd hit a chord, and the awareness felt strangely uncomfortable, as if something inside him would snap if she kept pushing.

But Lynda had decided to go for it. "What if . . ."

He cut her off. His wife had the infuriating ability to make him look at himself, even when the view was messy. He hated it and needed it. "What if what?"

She hesitated.

"Tell me. What if what?"

"What if you stopped being afraid?"

"Afraid? Afraid of what?"

"Oh, I don't know. Afraid of failing. Afraid of working at something that doesn't feel natural? Afraid of pushing yourself to become who you really want to be?"

"And what would that be?"

A sudden rush of emotion caught him off guard. The face of his father rose before him—the greater than life man he would never be. He could never fill the shoes of Daniel Reed—the words he'd told himself when he'd closed the door of his office before leaving for MonikerTech.

"I gotta go, Lynda." He'd had enough.

"I love you. I believe in you, Daniel, more than you believe in yourself. My prayer is that before you come home, you'll begin to trust the Daniel who won my heart." His wife's words hung in the air like the final note of a song.

Daniel turned off his phone. He wasn't sure how long he stood in silence in the hallway before he forced his thoughts back to his job, his responsibilities, and the long day that still lay ahead.

 **Bridge Builder Notes**

Hard questions demand thoughtful answers.

- What would you do if you weren't afraid?
- Who can you trust to show you the way?

CHAPTER 15

RETURN ON INVESTMENT

Daniel walked around the campus, weaving in and out of the breezeways between the five circular glass buildings that formed the perimeter of the campus. When he returned to go back into the meeting room, he realized he'd been gone for over an hour. Tammy had left, and Chris was talking to Chad Decker, Daniel's old college roommate and—to his astonishment—MonikerTech's CFO.

During his walk, Daniel had resigned himself to the fact that he would never have made the cut at MonikerTech, according to the standards Tammy had laid out. Chad Decker was not only a year younger than he was, but also had been the campus comedian and not a hard-charger like Daniel. Now he was MonikerTech's CFO. The realization was a hard pill to swallow.

"So I hear you're here to borrow our secret sauce," Chad chided after a few minutes of small talk. Daniel looked over to Chris who was rolling her eyes and nodding her head. She herded the group toward the table.

"Just the recipe—if I can." Daniel still couldn't believe that Chad was working for MonikerTech. If he'd been asked for a short list of potential Superb Communicator CFOs, Chad would have never crossed his mind. Yes, he was a likable guy with a story for everything to be sure, but a Bridge Builder? Obviously, Daniel was still missing something. "So, do you have any questions for me, old pal?"

"Just one. I'm trying to understand how such a concentrated corporate effort on communication development is even possible, sustainable, cost effective, or achievable. Doesn't all that effort deter attention and resources from the real business—you know, innovation, operations, research and product development, marketing, pricing, strategy, sales, mergers and acquisitions?"

"That's a common misconception," Chad answered as he slid into a chair between Daniel and Chris. "You and I know that companies with great products fail all the time—even the most innovative ones. Talented individuals with great potential hit the glass ceiling all the time." Chad paused when Daniel looked away. "Most of them can't figure out why— but we do."

Daniel met Chad's eyes again. He understood exactly what Chad was talking about. His previous company, one of the hottest startups in the Valley at the time Daniel joined the team, had slowly lost steam for no apparent reason in only a couple of years—and no one could tell him why.

They had the talent. They had several rounds of funding. They had the technology. Yet, younger companies were passing them by, and the company under his financial watch was no closer to becoming a key player in the industry than the day they opened the doors.

Daniel had seen the writing on the wall. No major player seemed interested in partnering with them or even acquiring them. Their investors had begun to direct their money elsewhere. No one talked about it aloud, but everyone knew that things needed to change or the money would eventually run out.

Chad couldn't have known how frustrated Daniel had been before accepting the interim CEO seat at BeyondYou. The truth was that when Paul came knocking, Daniel had come as close to prayer as life had ever pushed him. He either needed a way to help move the profit needle in the right direction, or he needed to begin planning his exit strategy.

"I understand what you're suggesting, Daniel," Chad said. Daniel barely remembered what he'd suggested until Chad brought it all back. "You've probably experienced times when training and development have become obstacles—barriers—to doing the real work, good work."

"Yes!"

"I have too—before coming to MonikerTech. And the point you made is valid. After all, we are in a business that makes money by selling real products that need to be conceived, designed, manufactured, and shipped."

"Yes, yes, and yes!" Those words had been his argument all along. Daniel could hardly believe he was talking to the same Chad he'd once known. It was as if he'd grown a new head on his shoulders.

"Can I share what I've learned in the last two years?" Chad waited for Daniel to respond.

"Yes, please."

"Training and development that is *reactionary* costs a lot of money and yields little, if any, return on investment." Chad grabbed the water bottle he'd carried with him into the room and took a long sip, letting Daniel sit with his statement. "On the other hand," he continued, "a training and development strategy that's part of the culture—part of the organization's DNA—is *sustainable*. It pays for itself."

"Explain *reactionary*." Daniel picked up his pen.

"Let me give you an example. Did Tammy talk to you about the bank where we met?"

"The Bank of CT, the terrorist?"

"CT—I knew her well. I was a loss mitigation analyst for a short stint after business school, and I had to deal with her more times than I care to remember. Now that bank is the perfect example of costly *reactionary* training and development.

"Every so often, management would get their hands slapped because we, the branch, weren't doing enough business or we were losing customers. I'm assuming that's what happened because the Corporate Suits would show up, and shortly afterward, everyone had to attend mandatory training, usually on Saturdays. After the training, it was back to business as usual—no follow up—until the Suits returned, or when one of the managers got replaced with another. And on and on the merry-go-round we went.

"Reactionary professional development is always a costly Band-Aid, usually to 'remedy' bad meetings, bad presentations and customer service, ineffective teamwork, sloppy communication that is misconstrued as sexual harassment, you name it."

"So how do you measure ROI?" Daniel interrupted.

Chad let out a hearty laugh. "I knew you were going to ask that. And to be frank, that's the hardest part for numbers guys like us. You can't measure ROI of a Bridge Builder culture with a spreadsheet or quantifiable metrics—not in the traditional sense. But make no mistake, the ROI is measurable—and it's not all the touchy-feely stuff I know you hate."

"You read my mind."

"I haven't forgotten my old roomy," Chad reached over and tapped Daniel's arm. "Seriously, the ROI is real. Internally, employee engagement is higher—and we do know that engaged employees work harder, stay longer, and contribute more to the bottom line. Externally, unsolicited client testimonials and referrals are not only at an all-time high, but they also paint a very clear picture.

"I can see you got the red binder. It's all there—assessments, spreadsheets, case studies," he paused. "I included your father's case study in there, too. It starts on page sixteen."

Daniel hated feeling exposed. Why hadn't he taken the time to review the case study? Clearly his head had been buried inside Excel spreadsheets for way too long. He opened the notebook and quickly scanned it. He didn't remember reading it, and he didn't have to admit it. His face told the story.

Apparently, Chris didn't need a confession. Instead, she decided it was time for a change of scenery. That could only mean one thing—a new lesson.

Daniel felt a rush of anticipation. He was just beginning to figure out how little time he had to learn what he knew he didn't know.

 **Bridge Builder Notes**

Chad says that reactionary professional development is costly when used to "remedy" poor results—bad meetings, bad presentations and customer service, ineffective teamwork, etc.

- Can you think of a time when you felt that your professional development was reactionary? Why?
- When was the last time you felt that your professional development was strategic?

CHAPTER 16

THE GREATEST BARRIER

The drive from MonikerTech to Coronado only took a few minutes. Daniel spent them mostly in silence, looking out the window of Chris's car. The drive seemed to relax him, draining away his defensiveness.

"The famous curved bridge." He commented on the design of the Coronado Bridge as they began the approach across the span.

"An 80-degree curve, in fact," Chris offered. "As you can imagine, I've been obsessed with bridges most of my life. When I first came to San Diego, I asked myself, wouldn't a straight line across the bay make more sense? Shorter distance. Cheaper to build and maintain. But as it turns out, the Coronado Bay isn't the only barrier. Engineers had to figure out a way to leave enough clearance for US Navy ships, which operate out of the San Diego Naval Station and must maintain regular access to the bay."

"Fascinating."

"Yes, the ideal bridge, which exists today, must be high enough for all US Navy ships to pass beneath, but not too steep for vehicles to ascend and descend. The bridge is a true testament that challenging barriers can be overcome."

Daniel sensed that Chris's words were intentional, as usual. This wasn't a random conversation. What did Tammy say? "Intention is the mark of a Bridge Builder."

"So what's the greatest barrier to becoming a Superb Communicator?" Daniel could hardly believe the question was coming from his lips.

"Ordinary communication."

"Of course." A hint of sadness edged his voice. The hallmark of his marriage for the past several years. Superficialities. Whatever came easily. Lynda had begged for more over and over again.

Neither Chris nor Daniel spoke for the remainder of the ride, which continued down Orange Street. When they reached the end of the road, Chris turned into the Ferry Landing parking lot and parked facing the San Diego Bay and downtown skyline. When Chris turned the engine off, Daniel broke the silence. "You're going to tell me what ordinary communication is—and why it's my greatest barrier, aren't you?"

"But you've heard it before." She smiled.

"From my father." Daniel sat back in the seat and stared out the window. "Funny thing. He probably died thinking I never listened to a word he said. But I actually did." Daniel was surprised by the sudden realization. "Even now, I can still hear him saying, 'Son, ordinary communication dwells deep in the abyss of *me, myself, and I.*'" Daniel echoed his father's words with all the drama he could muster, like an actor delivering a Shakespearean soliloquy. "'I want. I feel. I believe. I deserve. I'm offended. Daniel, my son, these sentiments are often rooted in ordinary—self-centered—communication.'"

Daniel paused and took a deep breath, preparing for the passionate finale. "'Ordinary communication is about noise. It's about talking without communicating. It's about data without story. It's about monologue—not dialogue. Ordinary communication rarely leads to connection.' And there you have it."

Daniel couldn't decide if cynicism or emotion was behind the edge in his voice. He wasn't sure he cared.

"Your father had a penchant for the theatrical when he was passionate about something, didn't he?" Chris's steady gaze and choice of words told Daniel she'd chosen to remain positive in spite of his caustic words.

"Yes he did."

"He was right. Most communication today lacks intention. We speak without thinking. We post our unedited thoughts for the world to see through social media. During conflict, we jump to conclusions and don't give others the benefit of the doubt. And we certainly get offended far too easily."

"He used to say that intentionality is hijacked by the modern tweet, Facebook update, text message, PowerPoint presentation, water cooler gossip session, and— 'Have It Your Way,' slogans."

Daniel turned toward the window and remained silent for a moment, as he connected all the dots. "Ordinary—you have no idea how much I've hated that word. You have no idea how much I hated my father using it as an adjective that applied to me."

"*Ordinary* applies to everyone—when intention goes out the window. Ordinary becomes our default."

"Even for you?"

She smiled. "Even for me."

"So how do I turn it around? How do I change?"

Chris had hoped to hear these words from Daniel by the end of the day if they were going to make real progress during his stay. He was ahead of schedule, and she couldn't be more thrilled. "Daniel, you already are changing!"

"So you can help me. You believe I have what it takes to be a Bridge Builder—and to build a company of Bridge Builders?"

"I wasn't too sure this morning, but I'm optimistic now." She smiled.

For the first time since he'd left home, Daniel also felt a sense of optimism as he looked into the eyes of his father's mentor. But somehow, he also knew she wasn't going to make change easy for him.

 **Bridge Builder Notes**

Chris says that ordinary communication—today's default form of communication that is marked by a lack of intention—is the greatest barrier to meaningful connection.

- Do you agree or disagree with this assessment?
- What communication barriers are currently keeping you from building better relationships at work or at home?

CHAPTER 17

LOSING THE ARMOR

Daniel relaxed in his chair and took a deep breath as he grabbed the menu, allowing himself to enjoy the sun, the breeze, and the view of the sailboats. He was glad Chris asked for outdoor seating.

Daniel couldn't remember the last time he'd allowed himself to be vulnerable, but he knew the time had come to learn. Through their meal, Daniel confessed that he was scared to death. That he didn't know how he was going to fill his father's shoes. That he hated being affected by comments of malicious bloggers. And that he didn't want to go down without a fight.

Bloggers and his harshest critics in the media didn't seem to care that he was listening. Daniel was learning firsthand the difference between ordinary and superb communication.

"It's all beginning to make sense now." Daniel paused.

"I sense there's a story. I'd love to hear it."

"When I graduated from business school, I received several offers. One of them was an executive position that offered me the potential to make my mark. Dad also made me an offer to come work alongside him."

"But you turned down his offer."

"Let's just say that we had some fundamental disagreements. He thought I needed to invest time growing as a communicator—by working my way up from the bottom. 'Getting to know my audiences,' I believe were his words. I disagreed." Daniel paused to compose himself. "What did he know? Of course, I knew he was The Great Daniel Reed, the rock star entrepreneur who wooed the world. Everyone knew that. But I wasn't him. And I convinced myself that his success was a combination of good instincts, timing, luck—and a set of talents I would never have. At the time it didn't make sense to me why he was placing so much emphasis on one single ability—or lack of ability—to be a stellar communicator like he was. So I expressed my opinion with a few expletives."

"What did he say?"

"He let me blow off steam, then explained that he didn't expect me to be his clone—that his desire was to give me a valuable gift. Then he said that there would always be a place for me at BeyondYou when I was ready."

"What did you say?"

"I walked out."

Silence hung in the air. Chris seemed to be waiting for Daniel to add to the discoveries he was making. "My father wanted me to become a Bridge Builder, didn't he?"

"I'm sure he did." Daniel could feel the compassion in her voice. "And I believe he knew you would come around eventually."

"Deep inside I did, too. We always think we have more time to build bridges, don't we? I just wish..." He stopped to regain his composure. After a long pause, he finished his thought. "I'd do things differently if I had a second chance."

"Daniel, I hope you don't mind me saying this—or find my words patronizing. I've never seen someone make as big a stride as fast as you have in such a short period of time, not in all my years of working with executives and organizations. Thank you for letting me in."

"Dad did say I was a fast learner." He smiled, realizing that this was the first day he had referred to his father as Dad—for a long time.

Talking about his father so candidly was not something Daniel was accustomed to doing. But he seemed to be under a vulnerability spell, so he kept sharing.

He told Chris how he'd managed to avoid presentations in high school, until he couldn't dodge that first dreaded college presentation. "Later, someone said I spoke so fast, he couldn't understand a word I said. Another classmate shared she counted seventy-five *umms*, then stopped counting.

"Then there was a company-wide survey when I was CFO. It was intended to gather employee feedback that could improve creativity and productivity. Several employees singled me out. One pointed out, in no uncertain terms, that I led meetings that sucked everyone dry of energy. Another one said that my presentations were too technical. Another one that I wasn't approachable."

Chris laughed. "Daniel, you're talking about presentation skills and communication skills that anyone can learn. And you *will* learn them—much more easily than you think. Trust me."

Time flew by in one of the most unexpected and encouraging conversations Daniel had ever had. He felt ready to dive in and learn all he could and tried to ignore the voice deep inside him that told him that he was a fraud and that, once again, he would fail.

And this time, he would lose more than just business opportunities.

Bridge Builder Notes

We always think we have more time to build bridges . . .

- What bridges have you postponed building to someone, thinking that one day you may get around to it?
- What communication skills do you already know you need to learn to become a more effective Bridge Builder?

CHAPTER 18

REALITY CHECK

Both Chris and Daniel agreed it was time to call it a day. On his way to the hotel, Daniel turned on his phone to find a missed call and message from Paul.

"Daniel, I just got off a conference call with the board. It seems that our constituents are more jumpy than we initially projected. I've taken the liberty to schedule a series of vision-casting presentations and meetings, starting a week from today. I know it's short notice, especially since you haven't met with the entire board and don't technically take BeyondYou's reins until next month. But we think it's a good idea to show investors, clients, and employees that BeyondYou is in good hands.

"I'll be out of reach for the next three days, but I'll touch base when I get back. Good thing you have the Bridge Builder's ear!"

Paul's voice projected its signature upbeat tone. But Daniel read between the words. The board was losing confidence.

It was up to Daniel to show them their trust was placed in the right man—but to first believe it himself.

Bridge Builder Notes

Newfound resolve can be fragile and must be protected.

- What's the danger of reading between someone's words?
- How do you protect your resolve when doubts creep in?

CHAPTER 19

U-TURNS

Daniel arrived back at the hotel mentally and emotionally exhausted. He lay down and fell asleep within a few minutes.

At one in the morning, he woke up with a vulnerability hangover.

As Daniel weighed his earlier conversation with Chris, followed by Paul's message, he cringed. There was nothing he hated more than employees bringing their personal issues to work. What had he been thinking? He was the CEO of BeyondYou, not an awkward teenager anxious about his first day of college.

What was he doing indulging in touchy-feely conversations when he should be thinking about preparing to face the board and investors? The more he thought about the things he'd said, the hotter he got. He'd barely had time to review the latest company financials and impact projections, let alone the production and product launch pipeline. How was he supposed to sift through all the data and prepare a proper analysis and strategy to convey confidence and competence before the upcoming board meeting?

This is ridiculous! I've got to regain control, and fast.

His mind raced, turning over the options that faced him. He decided to email Chris.

Chris,

I hope you get this email before we get started in the morning.

First, I want to apologize for dumping on you this afternoon. It was unprofessional. I don't want to waste your time. It won't happen again.

I want to conclude that conversation by admitting that I've been a dunce for the majority of my adult life. I was privileged to be the son of the great Daniel Reed and to learn from him. I chose to waste that opportunity—I get it. I can do nothing about it now, and I need to put that behind me and get on with the business of leading BeyondYou.

I would appreciate it if we can refocus and discuss how I can prepare for three types of communication needs coming up, namely delivering a vision-casting presentation, leading strategic planning meetings with my executive team, and developing a change communication strategy.

I believe those are my top priorities right now, and I'd be grateful if we can stay focused on those items for the remainder of my stay.

Daniel

Daniel reread the email twice, removing the fluff before hitting *Send*. It was important that he keep conversations brief, uncluttered, and moving forward. He felt good about the email, knowing it was time to stop playing games.

If the Bridge Builder couldn't help him to get ready to face the crisis at home, it was time to cut this little retreat short and call it quits.

Bridge Builder Notes

Vulnerability.

- How comfortable are you with it?
- How do you react after you've allowed yourself to be vulnerable at a deeper level—especially in professional situations?

CHAPTER 20

PERSPECTIVE

D aniel couldn't stop thinking about his upcoming board presentation. Since he couldn't sleep, he decided to work on his PowerPoint slides. He couldn't remember a time when he'd spent so many hours laboring over a presentation. By six in the morning, he'd narrowed the slides down to a total of forty-seven. He was confident that his investment of time would pay off, thinking that with Chris's help, he might just be able to hit it out of the park.

When he arrived at MonikerTech, he found Chris greeting a large gathering of people outside the auditorium. "Good morning, Daniel. I was waiting for you," she exclaimed over people's chatter and the music coming from the loudspeakers.

"Hi, did you get my email?"

"Yes, I did. Don't worry. We're on the same page." She smiled. "You know, Daniel, it's my experience that vulnerability—in communication and in general—is a needed medicine that often carries an aftertaste, particularly sour when taken for the first time. I'm certain you'll have this all figured out." She patted him on the shoulder, then gestured toward the auditorium. "We'll get started as soon as Michael's keynote is over."

Daniel felt as if he'd been punched in the gut. "Keynote? What keynote?"

"MonikerTech's first Bridge Builder Leadership Symposium starts today with Michael's keynote. We've been working on his presentation for a couple of weeks, and I'm looking forward to seeing him deliver it from the big stage. I included the program in the Blueprint I emailed you last night."

The Blueprint. The one I forgot to review.

Fortunately Daniel stopped himself before his confession reached his lips.

What else have you forgotten? If they only knew—vulnerability is the last thing I need right now.

He followed Chris to the front of the packed auditorium, facing the stage dead center. At least three hundred people had gathered in the room.

"Who are all these people?" Daniel whispered in her ear.

"MonikerTech's management and leadership team."

Great. A time waster. Is this event going to get in the way of you helping me?

Daniel hoped his irritation didn't show on his face. Michael was walking to the front of the stage, and Daniel could see the whites of his eyes. As usual, Michael was in charge. Every eye in the room was on him.

"Let me tell you a story . . .

"Once upon a time, two brothers who lived on adjoining farms fell into conflict. It was their first serious rift in forty years of farming side-by-side, sharing machinery, and trading labor and goods without a hitch.

"Then one day the long collaboration fell apart. It began with a small misunderstanding, and it grew into a major difference and finally exploded into an exchange of bitter words, followed by weeks of silence.

"One morning a knock came on the older brother's door. He opened it to find a man with a carpenter's toolbox. 'I'm looking for a few days work,' he said. 'Perhaps you might have a few small jobs here and there. Could I help you?'

"'Yes,' said the older brother. 'I do have a job for you. Look across the creek at that farm. That's my neighbor; in fact, it's my younger brother. Last week there was a meadow between us, but he took his bulldozer to the river levee and now there is a creek between us. Well, he may have done this to spite me, but I'll go him one better. See that pile of lumber curing by the barn? I want you to build me a fence—an 8-foot fence—so I won't need to deal with him any more.'

"The carpenter said, 'I think I understand the situation. Show me the nails and the post-hole digger, and I'll be able to do a job that pleases you.'

"The older brother had to go to town for supplies, so he helped the carpenter get the materials ready, and then he was off for the day. The carpenter worked hard all that day measuring, sawing, nailing.

"About sunset, when the farmer returned, the carpenter had just finished his job. The farmer's eyes opened wide, and his jaw dropped.

"In the location where he'd asked a fence to be built, a bridge stretched from one side of the creek to the other! It was a fine piece of work, including handrails and decorative millwork. Even more shocking was that his neighbor, his younger brother, was walking across the bridge, his hands outstretched.

"'You are a true brother to build this bridge after all I've said and done,' the brother on the bridge called out to the farmer.

"The two brothers met at the middle of the bridge, taking each other's hands. After a few minutes, they both turned to the carpenter as the farmer whispered, 'Thank you, Bridge Builder, for showing me a different way!'

Michael paused and looked around the auditorium. Daniel felt as if Michael were looking straight at him. Michael leaned in and lowered his voice, as if he were talking to a friend across the table, letting him in on a secret. "Now let me tell you why the story you just heard is not fiction—not for me. Not for us . . ."

Daniel looked around the room to observe the faces of MonikerTech employees, all hanging on their leader's every word. Daniel could see many of them taking copious notes, tweeting sound bites from Michael's message, or just nodding their heads. For the moment, Daniel forgot that the same Michael speaking to him from the stage was the man he had tried to avoid at every turn. Michael reminded Daniel of his father. Transparent. Humble. Passionate.

Michael went on to confess that he had lived the majority of his adult life as the brother from the story who had erected walls. He talked about having the good fortune of finding a friend who modeled a different way. "If today were my last day to leave a legacy with this business," he added, "I would spend it building a relationship—a bridge to someone I neglected—not a brand or a marketing campaign," said Michael.

Daniel opened his notebook and uncapped his pen, but captured by Michael's story, he found himself unable to write.

". . . We are not in the semiconductor business, though we design and manufacture the best semiconductors on the market today." Michael's words weren't lost on Daniel, for the first time since he'd arrived at MonikerTech. Daniel could sense his attitude changing, his suspicion slipping away. He found himself wanting to learn from a man who clearly commanded the respect of his company. He wanted to know how he could be that kind of leader, too.

"We are not in the innovation business, though innovation is synonymous with our name," Michael continued. "And we are not in the sales business, though our sales are projected to triple this year. We are and always will be in the people business . . ."

Daniel couldn't escape Michael's gaze. "My key message to you and the key message for this conference is this: Bridge Builders who intentionally reach the hearts and minds of people are MonikerTech's true competitive advantage."

And there it was, displayed on the enormous wide screen above Michael's head, the first of only four slides in Michael's presentation, spelling out Michael's secret sauce, what Daniel had been wanting to discover since he'd arrived at MonikerTech.

Of course.

Daniel couldn't help but chuckle at the irony of it all. It was the same message he had resisted time and time again when his father was alive.

Michael's next words provided the definitive blow to the pride that had driven Daniel from his father's office for the last time.

"At every turn, our business thrives on the watch of a Bridge Builder, and it will tumble at the feet of someone who refuses to be one."

Daniel felt the sting of Michael's words as if he were hearing them from the mouth of his own father, but this time with an uncanny clarity he had never sensed before. He felt as if he was finally waking up from a stupor, and the fog of his own stubbornness and pride were lifting.

Suddenly, Daniel felt a jolt of anxiety in the pit of his stomach at the thought that he could wake up in the morning having forgotten what he was experiencing. It had happened before, and he could never let it happen again.

He opened his notebook and began writing furiously in what his old psychology professor would have described as a stream of consciousness.

A second chance? Is it possible I have a second chance? On the watch of Bridge Builders, business will thrive. At the feet of self-centered people, business will tumble. That can't be me—not this time! I won't let that happen! Scared. Terrified. I need to become a Bridge Builder. I want to! How do I do that? Do I even have enough time? What are the next steps?

"Friends, this ain't a marketing slogan," Michael chided in his Texas twang, interrupting Daniel's thoughts. The room erupted with laughter. "Unless we can communicate with each other," he continued with a sense of urgency in his voice. "Unless we can build relationships with our customers. Unless we can connect with our partners—no innovation, no single piece of technology or product, and no clever marketing will ever take us where we want to go!"

Daniel knew it wasn't an accident that he'd been allowed to sit through this internal presentation. For the next fifteen minutes, he wrote as fast as he could as Michael spoke of *intentionality*, making choices that mattered.

"We must see our role as Bridge Builders first, *intentionally* removing—not erecting—communication barriers." He shared stories of MonikerTech's meteoritic growth and how as a team they had closed the gap with their competition—not just through innovation, outstanding products, and strategic marketing—but because their approach to overcoming communication barriers, internally and externally, enabled them to innovate faster, produce better products faster, and reach their customers and investors faster than anyone else.

Intentionality.

Lynda's face rose in his mind, and her words echoed in his memory. "Daniel, I love you, but you shut me out before a conversation begins. Years ago you won my love because you spoke straight to my heart. That Daniel seldom speaks to me any more. I'm praying he's the man who returns to our marriage."

Intentionality.

The energy in the room was electric. Much to his own chagrin, Daniel had to admit that Michael's keynote was worthy of the standing ovation it received.

I'm not even close to being ready to face my employees, much less my wife.

The thought flickered through Daniel's mind. But to his surprise, he was able to quickly dismiss it. For the moment, what preoccupied his mind was much more profound. As he scanned through the scribbles in his notebook, he knew it was time to decide: was he going to start acting like a Bridge Builder—at least a Bridge Builder in training who was willing to learn?

Daniel knew one thing for sure—he'd run out of options and he'd run out of time. If he could muster the courage to swallow his pride, he'd walk up to Michael and ask him for help.

 **Bridge Builder Notes**

Michael's perspective is that our work and profitable relationships thrive on the watch of a Bridge Builder and tumble at the feet of someone who refuses to be one.

- Where have you seen profitable relationships thrive on the watch of a Bridge Builder?
- Where have you seen profitable relationships tumble at the feet of someone who refuses to build bridges?
- "We're in the people business." Is it a mere cliché or a timeless principle?

CHAPTER 21

MEDICINE

A re you comparing yourself to Michael?" Chris's words startled Daniel. He was standing in the lobby, looking toward the stage, where a few lingering participants were gathered around Michael. "I'm asking because you look like you've stopped breathing."

Daniel could tell she wasn't really asking. For a second, she sounded like Lynda, who could anticipate his thoughts and knew what he was going to say even before he did.

"It actually happened to me once, you know. I stopped breathing." Chris was standing next to him, and Daniel knew he wasn't going to escape the story she was about to tell. "It was during my last year of college, and I decided to join the debate team. I was doing pretty well until Marcia Barnes came along. She was eloquent and electrifying. As I watched her take the podium, as I waited for my turn, I stopped breathing. I was in awe of her skills, knowing deep inside I could never match them. I passed out."

"Really?" Daniel pretended to be interested.

"Yes, it's true. And I don't want you to pass out." She winked.

Thank you for your concern, Lady Bridge Builder, but I don't know what you're talking about . . . He caught himself and cut off the negative thoughts. He needed to stop fighting, right then and there, to stop taking one step forward and two steps back. He opted for honesty. "You're right. Michael was great—truly phenomenal."

"Take him off the pedestal, Daniel." Her tone was stern, yet maternal.

"What?" Daniel broke into nervous laughter.

"And one more thing," Chris said, this time more gently.

Daniel took a deep breath. "Am I going to like hearing it?"

"Probably not. But I'll only say it once." Daniel forced himself to keep an open attitude.

"Take your critics off the pedestal as well." Daniel fought the urge to jump in and defend himself. "Stop bowing down at the altar of others' opinion and approval—or you'll never be the leader you can be or the Bridge Builder you want to be."

Daniel knew Chris was right—just like Lynda was. Chris's words were awful-tasting medicine, but he needed it. Daniel had the feeling that this wouldn't be the last time he would have to take it.

"I get what you're saying, but how can I ever compete with that?" He pointed toward the stage. "How can I ever command the attention and respect of BeyondYou's leaders like Michael does?"

Chris turned toward the stage and waved to Michael. "Why don't you ask him yourself?"

Bridge Builder Notes

Honest feedback from a trusted mentor is medicine.

- Bowing down at the altar of opinion and approval—how much of a challenge is this for you?
- Are mental comparisons part of your internal dialogue?
- How are they affecting your ability to reach your goals?

CHAPTER 22

HUMILITY

Daniel didn't appreciate being put on the spot, but he'd become accustomed to Chris forcing him to step out of his comfort zone. Still, he could feel his heart beating faster when he saw Michael approaching. He wasn't ready to face him without his self-defensive armor.

Breathe, Daniel. You can do this.

"I think we're off to a great start, don't you think?" Michael asked Chris enthusiastically as he joined them.

"Most definitely. You were great up there, Michael. Daniel and I were just talking about it."

Apparently Daniel's conspiracy theory about Michael's intentions were wearing off, and he was being transformed by Bridge Builder talk. The fact was that he couldn't agree with Chris more. He moved past his hesitation and stepped into the conversation and uncharted territory. "Yes, truly phenomenal, Michael. Thank you for allowing me to take part."

Michael's eyes widened. Apparently he was as surprised as Daniel was by his uncharacteristic sincerity and humility.

"In fact," Daniel couldn't seem to stop himself, "I was wondering if we could reschedule Friday's meeting. I'd like to pick your brain and tap into your wisdom sooner if possible."

Is it possible that I actually mean it?

Michael turned to Chris, seemingly stumped by the change in Daniel's brashness from the day before. He stood quietly, as if pondering the question and whether he wanted to forgive and forget.

The silence was excruciating for Daniel. "You know, I don't know what I was thinking. Let's just forget the whole thing."

Michael cut him off, giving Daniel a hearty pat on the arm.

"Let's do it, Son." Michael's voice was edged with enthusiasm.

Daniel turned to Chris and found a comforting smile and a friendly wink. Daniel pulled out his phone and quickly consulted his calendar as Michael interrupted him. "That is, if you don't mind following me around."

"What do you mean?

"I'm participating in a few breakouts and activities today. I'm leading a campus tour tomorrow. You can tag along. Then we can grab dinner. What do you say?"

A familiar rush of negativity flooded his thoughts, but this time he cut off the flow. He put his best foot forward, using what he'd learned from the "assume positive intentions" talk.

Michael is doing me a favor by including me.

He thanked Michael, projecting as much confidence as he could. Neediness was something he couldn't stomach—in himself or others. So he chose to avoid eye contact with Chris, in case she threw him one of Lynda's maternal "I'm-so-proud-of-you" looks.

"So what's next?" Daniel asked.

"Who do you think you are?" said Michael.

"Excuse me?" Daniel stiffened for a second.

"Lighten up! That's the theme of this afternoon's sessions—*Who Do You Think You Are?*"

Daniel tried to keep his face from reflecting the feeling of horror that had hit him in the stomach. "If we start singing 'Kumbaya,' I'm taking the first plane back to . . ." He stopped cold. "Did I just say that out loud?"

The three of them erupted in laughter. "Yes, you most certainly did," Michael answered. "And let me be the first to say, Daniel, that it's refreshing to hear you say what you're actually thinking."

Daniel realized that this was the first time since he'd arrived that Michael had called him by his name. Today was a new day, and he decided to give himself permission to enjoy the rest of it. After all, he had the rest of the week to work with Chris on his presentation.

 Bridge Builder Notes

Asking for help is bridge building.

- How difficult is it for you to admit you need help?
- When was the last time you asked for help from someone who you perceived as your competition?
- When was the last time you asked for help from someone who intimidated you?

CHAPTER 23

UNEXPECTED POTHOLES

During the break, Daniel walked out to the courtyard and turned on his phone to find three missed calls and two voice messages, one from Lynda and one from Paul.

"Babe, Paul's called me twice to see if something's wrong with your phone. He needs to talk to you. Sounded serious."

Next call. "Morgan, our top investor, who also sits on the board, is threatening to pull out. Call me as soon as you get this."

And I thought this was going to be a fun day.

Reluctantly, Daniel dialed Paul's number and braced himself for the worst as Paul picked up. "Should I pack my bags and head back?"

"It's not that simple, Daniel. You're not BeyondYou's CEO yet—not on paper . . ."

Daniel cut him off. "What are you saying?" He felt a cold chill run down his spine. It hadn't been his idea to postpone the formal CEO installation formalities until after Bridge Builder training. If he wasn't CEO of BeyondYou or the CFO of his previous employer, he was technically unemployed and probably unemployable.

In a nanosecond, Daniel could see the writing on the wall: "Sorry, Daniel. We acted rashly—contrary to what your father would have done. We appreciate your willingness to quit your job on a day's notice and take us at our word that a contract would be waiting for you after your Bridge Builder retreat—but we changed our minds. It's not you. It's us." *Breathe.*

Daniel's mind was racing as he prepared a comeback. "Forget about your offer. I don't need your permission to take what's rightfully mine. I'm my father's only heir, and I can guarantee you that I can find a way to exercise my options even before his estate is settled . . ."

Paul's voice brought him back. "Daniel, are you there?"

"Sorry. Can you repeat what you said? I lost you for a second."

"I said that there's nothing you can do here for the moment, not until you're officially installed next week." Daniel felt a twinge of relief. "Morgan is playing hardball. He's bargaining for the chairman seat, and he's trying to back us into a corner. Your father would have been appalled!"

"Do we have a choice?"

"Well, as it turns out, I just finished reading a message from a potential investor who would not only make it easy for us to let Morgan go, but also would be a terrific long-term strategic partner as well." Paul's signature joviality had returned, but Daniel cut him off.

"Who?"

"I don't want to say just yet. Don't want to jinx it. He's not able to talk today, but we have a conference call scheduled for tomorrow. But I can say that it will definitely come down to you."

"Explain." Daniel's anxiety began to boil again.

"He's not the silent partner type. He's hands-on. He'll want to make sure you'll be able to work together. But getting him on board would be like hitting the jackpot. So keep learning how to build bridges. That's exactly what will make a difference when you finally step in."

"And if he doesn't think we can work together—then what?"

"Let's cross that bridge when we get to it—no pun intended."

Daniel hung up the phone. His heart was racing. Only one person could help him regain perspective. He needed to make a call, and it would have to be quick.

 **Bridge Builder Notes**

Building bridges is about overcoming obstacles.

- What obstacles do you face that necessitate strong bridge building skills?
- Who do you call when you need help to regain perspective?
- How does he or she help you reconsider your perspective?

CHAPTER 24

CORRECTION

By the time Daniel finished telling Lynda about the keynote, his conversation with Michael, and the call with Paul, he'd convinced himself that following Michael around all day would be counterproductive. "I can't sit around all day in meetings. I can't even remember what I wanted to talk to Michael about. I won't be able to focus—besides, I hate meetings!" He took a deep breath. "What do you think?"

"Quick story," she said.

Here we go.

Daniel rolled his eyes, knowing too well that she'd been saving this one for such an occasion, but he couldn't help smiling, thinking of her beaming brown eyes and the dimple-to-dimple smile that melted his heart.

"A golfer is standing in the middle of a sand trap, preparing to hit the ball. He swings and misses the ball, but he manages to hit the anthill, killing hundreds of ants. He swings and misses the ball again, but he kills a few hundred more ants. After a few more swings and dead ants, one of the ants turns to another ant and says, 'If we want to survive, we better get on the ball.'"

Reluctantly, Daniel chuckled for her benefit, though he knew exactly what she meant. There was nothing he could do about Morgan, about Paul, or about the mysterious investor. One thing and one thing alone remained under his control—his commitment to become a Bridge Builder once and for all. In the process, he also was committing to become the man of courage he'd always secretly wanted to be—and the man he hoped would return home to Lynda.

 **Bridge Builder Notes**

In the midst of uncertainty, we can still build bridges.

- What is *out* of your control at the moment?
- What is *within* your control to do?

CHAPTER 25

WHO DO YOU THINK YOU ARE?

S oon after Daniel began following Michael around the symposium, he realized this wasn't just another professional development event like the dozens of other business and technology conferences he'd attended over the years. For one, he wasn't going to be able to blend into the background until Michael found time to talk to him. And the breakout sessions were definitely nothing like the ones he loathed, including sessions he'd led himself.

No, Daniel wasn't going to be sitting in the back of a darkened room, returning emails from his phone while a monotone, uninspiring presenter cycled through PowerPoint slides or spewed data points he could have read on his own. Instead, he found himself engaged by the environment and strangely irritated by the fact that he was being drawn in.

Daniel wasn't used to being part of an engaged culture or energy-charged meetings, where people seemed inspired by opposing points of view and disagreement. It was both exhilarating to witness productive debate and dialogue—and infuriating at the same time. The budding Bridge Builder within him was at odds with the Daniel who wasn't quite ready to move on. The latter found himself wishing he could witness boring, trite communication—the type he'd grown accustomed to, secretly hoping he'd find a reason to say, "Aha! I knew it—mediocrity lives here too!"

No such luck. In fact, he was learning that the Bridge Builder cultural phenomenon extended beyond the San Diego campus. Managers and executives who made up MonikerTech's leadership team had come from around the country and abroad to participate in three days of real work, creative work, innovative work—under their shared identity as Bridge Builders.

"So this is what Superb communication looks like," Daniel commented in the few minutes he had to interact with Michael. But Michael countered, reminding him that effective communication was never about perfection.

"Yes, I know. It's about intention," Daniel finished the sentence, which inspired Michael to raise his hand, inviting a high-five. Reluctantly, Daniel obliged. But he wasn't yet ready to admit that what he was witnessing was sustainable. So many individuals with diverse personalities, expertise, and perspectives working as one—while still being able to further their personal goals and initiatives? No way.

By the end of the day, Daniel was mentally exhausted after observing strategy sessions and participating in creative meetings. He was ready to call it a day when he noted a teal-colored band on Michael's wrist. He suddenly realized he'd seen people wearing the bands since he'd arrived at MonikerTech. "What's the band about?" He pointed to Michael's wrist.

Michael extended his arm. "I'm a Bridge Builder," he said, reading the inscription. "We challenge each other with a follow-up question, 'Who do you think you are?' Our answer shows what we believe, how we listen, how we act, how we talk, and how we lead. So what about you, Daniel? Who do you think you are?"

Daniel froze. That was the question, after all, wasn't it? Michael reached out and took Daniel's hand and pressed something into it.

"Take it, Daniel. Consider it a gift." Michael smiled, then turned and walked away.

Daniel knew what Michael had placed in his hand. He slid it into his pocket and headed back to his room.

Bridge Builder Notes

You are—and communicate like—who you think you are.

- Who do you think you are?
- Is that the person you want to be?

CHAPTER 26

VISUAL AIDS

The next morning Daniel arrived late for breakfast—barely on time to join Michael on a tour of the MonikerTech campus with three prospective investors. The group was standing and talking by the window of the main lobby where Daniel had first met Chris.

Daniel was less than thrilled to join a show-and-tell tour. He was too anxious about his upcoming presentations, the fact that he hadn't had time to prepare properly, and the nagging thought that he hadn't heard from Paul yet. But Chris noticed his apparent anxiety and appeased him, reminding him that they had a formal coaching day ahead as soon as the tour was over and that watching Michael interact with investors was a profitable investment of time.

Daniel admitted to himself that she had a point as he joined the group. Michael was in rare form, gearing up like an eager kid anticipating a day at Disneyland. It was a side of Michael that Daniel hadn't seen before. He reminded him of himself as a young boy, waiting to show off his newest Lego creation to anyone willing to see it. Daniel could tell that Michael was anxious to get started and was beginning the introductions already.

Arav, an affable Indian investor, had just arrived from New York. A man wearing animal skin boots, whose name Daniel forgot the second Michael said it, had just arrived from Dallas. And Leticia, a stylish woman with a Spanish accent, had come from a South American country Daniel forgot as well. *Note to self: Listen!*

As Michael led everyone through the glass doors to the courtyard, Daniel couldn't escape the fact that Michael's passion and enthusiasm were rubbing off on his guests, whose cool demeanors were transforming right before his eyes. Their comments revealed that they had one thing in common: they had read the *Forbes* article featuring the MonikerTech campus. Immediately Daniel chided himself for not reading it.

In a side conversation, Chris explained that Michael Thompson had designed the campus as a tangible visual aid of their Bridge Builder culture and shared identity. Not surprising. Everyone who knew him—fans and critics—agreed that Michael's extraordinary success stemmed from the fact that he never reinvented the wheel, so to speak. Instead, he improved tested principles and launched them with his own unique brand of jet fuel. For Michael, innovation and leadership were all about synthesizing the best of ideas to create something uniquely powerful and useful. The *Forbes* article had dubbed him the King of the Mash-Up.

Michael kept the pace brisk as they walked through the courtyard, talking the entire time, pointing out features of the buildings that were designed to tell the story of their corporate culture. Michael was convinced—and cited the research to back him—that employees who worked united by a shared identity and supported by an intentional culture outperform those who don't. "A shared identity," he explained, "facilitates productive dialogue and faster resolution of conflict."

"Interesting," Arav nodded.

"When employees feel united by the vision of what they can achieve together, they keep communication channels flowing smoothly," Michael said. "This campus is a constant visual aid of our vision and culture."

Daniel kept his eyes fixed on Michael, as if he were trying to detect the exact formula behind his legendary ability to dazzle investors. "Team members can't become communication bottlenecks if they see themselves as Bridge Builders."

"Good point," said Arav.

"Clearly, not everyone needs to redesign a campus from the ground up to keep a shared identity in front of everyone," blurted the cowboy.

"We're not everyone," answered Michael without missing a beat.

The group chuckled, but not the cowboy.

"You told us from day one that MonikerTech's culture is crucial to the bottom line," the cowboy interrupted. "I don't know that I would have voted to make this kind of investment into a building project." Daniel perked up. The cowboy seemed to be reading his mind, and he could hardly wait to see what Michael would say. The cowboy finished his statement. "But it takes guts to invest in 'what's important' before 'what's urgent' gets in the way."

"Ha! You read the article," Michael interjected.

"Who hasn't?" the cowboy responded.

Daniel looked away. He felt a sense of relief when Chris handed everyone a sleek booklet with the fully illustrated story of the campus. He followed Michael's lead, turning to the campus diagram.

Five circular glass buildings formed the circumference of the campus, each dedicated to one of the five Principles of Bridge Builder Communication.

As the group walked through the shining glass doors of the first building, an enormous sign behind the reception area greeted them— THINK LIKE A BRIDGE BUILDER.

"Ladies and gentlemen, this is MonikerTech's first guiding principle," Michael announced.

As they walked through the sleek marble tile hallways, Michael explained that each building, just like the one they were touring, showcased one of five guiding principles—from the dynamic lobby multimedia displays to signage to décor—every space a canvas for education or inspiration.

"If you argue for your limitations, you get to keep them," flashed in a digital display. Another read, "I'm a Bridge Builder," followed by faces of employees. Other displays included instructional tips like "Before your next meeting, ask yourself: what story do I need to tell?"

After walking through the state of the art meeting rooms, Michael led the group to the glass elevator that took them to the third floor. The back door opened into one of the curved bridges that connected the buildings and completed the perfect circumference around a ring of courtyards that surrounded the atrium.

"The design communicates that Bridge Builder Leadership and Communication isn't a linear process. It's an ongoing discipline that involves constant learning and practice."

Standing on top of the bridge, the group paused and quieted as they took in the 360-degree view of the MonikerTech campus. "The Catalyst Atrium—the heart of the campus," Michael stated as he pointed to the pentagon shaped atrium in the center of the campus, "is where creativity, innovation, and community take place." Each story is dedicated to one of the three foundational attitudes that support all Bridge Builder Communication: empathy, authenticity, and respect.

The cowboy and Arav walked to the opposite side, taking pictures with their phones while Chris answered questions for Leticia.

"What do you think?" Michael startled Daniel, who hadn't noticed that Michael had moved near him.

"I don't know what to say. Seems so . . ." Daniel hesitated, "so over the top."

Michael let out a hearty laugh. "I'm sure you're not the only one who thinks that. But you're the first one to say it to my face."

Daniel felt relieved that Michael took his frankness in stride. It was a refreshing invitation to be himself. "I get that you want to be intentional. I get that you're not just paying lip service to an abstract ideal. But is this all necessary to support a Bridge Builder culture?"

"Maybe. Maybe not." Michael paused, turning to look out at the campus as if admiring his creation. "This investment isn't just about me or another corporate culture, Daniel. It's about a much bigger vision, the vision that a culture of Bridge Builders can lead the way . . ."

Daniel cut him off. "Lead the way in profits?" Daniel didn't even try to hide his incredulity, which didn't seem to affect Michael in the least.

"Lead the way in changing the world," he said with a laugh.

"That's quite a vision for a semiconductor company, don't you think?"

"It is." Michael smiled, looking over Daniel's shoulder to find his group waiting at the end of the bridge. Daniel looked at Michael, noticing a spark in his eyes he hadn't seen before. It wasn't the spark of a man who dazzles investors for a living. It wasn't the spark of a man who sells technology for a living. Daniel recognized it—a spark he'd seen only once before in his life.

Michael interrupted Daniel's thoughts. "If I can say one thing with certainty, it's that vision leaks. If you don't work to maintain and grow it, you lose it. And I just can't afford to let that happen here." Michael patted Daniel on the arm then walked to meet the rest of the party.

Vision leaks.

Daniel sank to the rear of the group and followed for the remainder of the tour, typing the principles he was discovering into his phone. More than once, sadness swept over him, as he noted the spark in Michael's eyes. Until now, he'd only seen it in one other man—his father. He'd been the only person Daniel knew who so decisively wanted to change the world—through his work and through his life.

He thought of BeyondYou and Paul and the board—the panic that motivated their request to ask him to step in as CEO. They thought they needed another Daniel Reed, so they asked his son without vetting him—seemingly not caring that he wasn't ready.

Daniel knew it. His father knew it. And the board must have known it.

Daniel didn't know enough about the BeyondYou culture, but one thing was clear—without his father and their former leader at the helm, vision was leaking and something needed to be done.

Daniel knew he didn't have Michael's funding or the audacity to build a monumental visual aid to keep his father's vision alive, but he knew one thing for sure—he, too, wanted to live with a vision to change the world.

Bridge Builder Notes

"Vision doesn't stick; it doesn't have natural adhesive. Instead, vision leaks." —**Andy Stanley**

- What's your vision?
- How do you keep it from leaking?
- What comes to mind when reading these words: "It takes guts to invest in 'what's important' before 'what's urgent' gets in the way"?

CHAPTER 27

RELUCTANT PRESENTER

W hen the tour was over, Chris led Daniel through the atrium and into what she called "The War Room." The large, sleek room was encased in glass walls, except for a single whiteboard wall that faced a living-room style sitting area with blue leather couches and chairs.

"Let's not start with the presentation to the board yet. Let's start with your presentation to BeyondYou's employees." Chris interrupted Daniel, who had quickly slid into a chair, opened his laptop, and was focused on his PowerPoint deck. Chris knew Daniel had been tinkering with slides for his upcoming Board presentation for the last two days. By her estimation, he had close to seventy slides. Starting the coaching session there would be a complete waste of time. They needed to start from scratch. "Tell me about the presentation to the employees."

"Well, it's more like a roadshow," he said. She could see the annoyance on his face. "One presentation, delivered multiple times at various locations. If I understand this right, I'm supposed to—never mind." He closed his laptop.

Chris was about to ask him to describe his personal goals for the presentation, but he cut her off. "It's the board's idea, not mine. As you know, I hate presenting. I'm a numbers guy, not a presenter. I realize that this is going to be part of my job now, but I think my time is better spent working on strategy and the big presentations for the board and investors, instead of spending all this time preparing for small presentations, no offense."

"None taken," Chris smiled, already aware that Daniel was still not thinking like a Bridge Builder or seeing his communication in terms of his audience. She wasn't surprised. It was her experience that the concept was foreign to most communicators. Daniel was no different, despite all he'd heard for the last two days. Now it was time to put theory into practice. She realized that the journey might feel to him like walking a marathon in a new pair of dress shoes.

The fact was that Daniel was still defaulting to an ordinary communication pattern, seeing his presentations as mere formalities in a corporate culture. From her vantage point, Daniel wasn't yet considering BeyondYou's culture and the audiences he would soon face.

"I actually feel sorry they have to sit through a highly technical presentation," he admitted.

Bingo! He finally said it.

As a numbers guy, used to seeing himself as a technical presenter, Daniel exemplified the tragic yet commonplace practice of *ordinary*, everyday communicators: failing to communicate with the audience.

The task was clear: Chris had to help Daniel shift his focus from himself, his strategy, and his data and help him redirect his focus to the needs of his audience.

Chris had learned long ago that attempting to build a bridge by fighting the barrier—trying to change her audience's mind—is like attempting to build a bridge to the moon. Arguing Daniel's points just would not work.

Building a bridge to Daniel's heart and mind—that's what she needed to do. If she succeeded, Daniel would not only feel better about his presentation and presenter role, but he also would learn that his audience wanted to be as excited as he was about his data. He simply had to build a bridge to where they were.

"Do you mind if we brainstorm for a while?" asked Chris, walking to the whiteboard and uncapping a marker.

"Sure."

She read the resignation in Daniel's face but kept moving forward. "So why should your audience care?" she asked, drawing a big circle with the word *WHY* in the center.

"They don't really care," Daniel stated, reminding Chris of the face of her frequently pouting teenage son.

"Alright." She drew another circle connected to the first. *DON'T CARE,* she wrote, and then added a new circle connected to the first. "Let's assume they do care. Why would they?" she asked again.

"I'm their new boss. They're forced to care," he offered.

FORCED, Chris wrote inside the circle. "Ok, let's keep going." She drew another circle connected to the first. Why else should they care?"

"I guess my data and approach can impact their departmental strategy and the future of their business unit."

"Does it?"

"Yes. Yes it does," he admitted as his eyes widened. "Bottom line, anything I say and do can impact their jobs."

Chris detected the *"aha moment"* she'd been hoping for. A rapid fire of questions and circles continued until a web suggesting various paths emerged until Daniel's answers began to flow more quickly.

"They also should care because my insights and leadership approach can impact their decisions. The data I share will paint a picture about the future of the company and the products and services they manage."

And there it was. Chris could see it in Daniel's eyes; the shift was taking place. A bridge had begun to form in his imagination.

Preparing his presentation—the first step toward building a bridge to his audience—to Daniel's surprise—was beginning to become a fun and creative process, once his focus shifted from himself to his audience. Daniel was beginning to admit that he'd never considered who his audience was—what they cared about, what they wanted to hear, what they didn't need to hear. He was able to acknowledge that they had the right to be concerned about his ability to lead and were probably as scared about the future as he was.

Daniel finally was beginning to say that he wanted—more than anything—to earn his audience's trust. He wanted them to understand that he would bring passion not only for the work his father began, but also skills and insights that would benefit BeyondYou—if they were willing to partner with him.

For the next several hours, Chris led Daniel through a brainstorming session that focused on the needs of his audience. Then she switched gears to the story Daniel wanted to communicate.

She challenged Daniel to come up with a single moral to his story— the bottom line he wanted his audience to remember from his message. This proved to be a time-consuming process, because Daniel wasn't used to synthesizing information into one key statement that encapsulated all the ideas he wanted to share. Chris handed him the marker, and Daniel took her place—writing and rewriting his message.

They talked about what pieces of data were valuable for them at this point in the process and which were best suited for subsequent meetings.

In less than eight hours, Daniel went from being a reluctant presenter to becoming a budding Bridge Builder, who, without realizing it, had incorporated Bridge Builder principles and Bridge Builder Communication elements.

With Chris's help, Daniel constructed a presentation that told a personal **Story** that took into account BeyondYou's story.

He kept only the information that was **Useful** to them, removing technical jargon and details that weren't relevant to the audience at that point in time.

He discovered, in the process of asking and answering the hard questions, that he had genuine **Passion** to connect with his audience, to lead BeyondYou, and to partner with BeyondYou's team members to continue the work his father had started.

As he kept his audience in mind all day, Daniel discovered a new sense of **Empathy** for what they were going through. They, too, had lost their leader and hero. He needed to look them straight in the eye. For this particular presentation, PowerPoint slides would present a barrier to the personal connection he needed to establish with them.

Daniel practiced his presentation half a dozen times without further complaints. Viewing his video recordings with his Bridge Builder self-assessment in hand, he identified areas of improvement. He realized that hard data was not as essential to being perceived as a **Reliable** leader for this particular presentation. Authenticity, transparency, humility, and passion were his highest priorities for the moment.

By the end of the day, Daniel had discovered **Brevity**. He saw that fluff, data overload, and pretentiousness distracted from his core message and call to action.

"I can't believe it." Daniel flopped down on his chair as the day came to a close. "Daniel Reed is becoming a Bridge Builder at last," he said. "**S**tory. **U**sefulness. **P**assion. **E**mpathy. **R**eliability. **B**revity. SUPERB!"

"You're thinking like a Bridge Builder. You're talking like a Bridge Builder. That's two of the five principles, Daniel. You can do this!"

For the first time since Chris had met Daniel, she saw passion and confidence in his eyes.

"You know, Chris, my father knew I could do this. I was too scared to want to find out what *this* even was. But for the first time in my life, I know I can be a Bridge Builder. And I know it will change my life."

 **Bridge Builder Notes**

Why? Start here.

- Why should your audience care about your message?
- Why do you want them to care?

CHAPTER 28

SOUL SEARCHING

D aniel declined the shuttle back to his hotel, where he was scheduled to meet Michael for dinner. He had an hour to kill and decided, instead, to take on the one-mile waterfront hike and enjoy the cool breeze and the sunset that had begun to creep in on the other side of the harbor.

The faces of BeyondYou's Executive Team members flashed through his mind as he remembered the meet-and-greet gathering in Paul's office the day Paul gave Daniel his father's letter.

Ron, the quiet but affable CFO had welcomed him with a warm smile. Marcy, the enthusiastic VP of Sales and Marketing, had startled him with a maternal hug and thanked him for joining the team. Sheryl, the self-effacing chief operations officer, had encouraged him by confessing that fifteen years prior, when she stepped in as COO, only Daniel Reed, Sr., thought she was the right fit for the job. And Brian, the chief visionary officer, had greeted him with a rock-solid handshake and pat on the arm.

"I do have allies," Daniel whispered, a sudden realization that his father's team members, despite their apprehensions about his ability—had made a choice to build bridges to him.

The insight shamed him.

Daniel stopped by a bench that overlooked the harbor. He sat down and fixed his eyes on the navy ship heading in the direction of the Coronado Bridge in the distance. He remembered Chris's story.

The ideal bridge must be high enough for all US Navy ships to pass beneath, but not too steep for vehicles to ascend and descend. It's a true testament that challenging barriers can be overcome.

He reflected on how much time and energy he'd spent thinking about himself, his agenda, his critics, and his insecurities, and how little time he'd spent thinking about the needs of his stakeholders and how to be an advocate for them. His attitude had become his greatest barrier. But he was no longer fighting for his limitations—he was overcoming his barriers.

He opened the leather journal, uncapped his pen, and turned to an empty page. He had no sooner written the words, "It's not about me," when he heard an unmistakable *ding*, announcing that a text message from Paul had arrived.

He pulled out his phone, and his heart sank as he read, "Call me if you're sitting down."

 **Bridge Builder Notes**

Bridges are built by many.

- Who are your allies?
- "It's not about me." How can this personal realization be a game changer?

CHAPTER 29

PLAN B

I'm sitting down," Daniel said as soon as Paul answered the phone. Daniel shifted his weight on the bench, fixing his eyes on a cargo ship loaded with hundreds of metal containers. He was surprised by the sense of calm he felt.

"We'll be in San Diego tomorrow morning." Paul's matter-of-fact tone was hard to read.

"Who's 'we'?" Daniel interrupted as calmly as he could, although he noticed his heart was beating faster.

"Still working out the details. A handful of board members," Paul hesitated. "Enough for a quorum."

"A quorum. That means you plan to vote on something. Tomorrow?" Daniel stood up and leaned over the metal rail. For a moment he thought he might throw up.

"We may have to . . ."

Daniel cut him off. "So what's going on? What can't wait till next week's board retreat? Why can't I just fly back?"

This time Paul cut Daniel off. "Calm down. We have a window of opportunity to meet with the investor I talked to you about. He's in San Diego for two more days before he leaves the country for I don't know how long. We may be able to secure a meeting."

Daniel cut him off again. "When? And who are we talking about?"

Paul paused. "I'm emailing you all the details. Could be Friday. Maybe tomorrow afternoon. We're waiting to hear back."

Daniel rubbed his temples. He could feel a tension headache gripping the base of his neck. "So what do you need from me?"

"Nail your presentation." Paul's jovial tone was back. "You probably already know this, but this meeting is about the new story of BeyondYou—and the passion you bring to its next chapter."

"Anything else?"

"Well," Paul hesitated.

"What?"

"It'd be great if *you* could run the meeting. Showcasing your leadership would speak volumes."

Daniel paused. He was hugely grateful that Paul hadn't Skyped him and couldn't see the terror that was likely written all over his face. "No problem."

"I'm emailing you everything you need. Remember, if this investor joins us, it'll be because he can work with you. No pressure."

"Yeah. No pressure."

Bridge Builder Notes

Expect the unexpected.

- Was there a time when you wished you had prepared a plan B?
- Sometimes we need someone to push us outside of our comfort zone. Who does that for you?

CHAPTER 30

LEGACY

Daniel arrived at the hotel restaurant before Michael. They'd agreed to meet for dinner at a secluded table next to the fountain. He didn't know exactly how the conversation would go or even what he wanted to ask Michael, but he didn't want to be the focus of attention if anyone in the room recognized them.

When Michael arrived, he greeted Daniel with his signature energy, but he looked tired.

After looking over the menu and deciding that neither of them was really hungry, they ordered an appetizer and drinks. Daniel resisted the urge to jump into business talk. But not Michael.

"Shoot—any question at all. This is your meeting." Michael turned off his phone and reached into the jacket he'd draped over one of the empty chairs as he slid the phone into a pocket. "I'm all ears."

Daniel hesitated. He'd almost forgotten he was the one who requested to move his meeting from Friday until now. By now, he should have been used to feeling unprepared, but the realization that he didn't know how to start the conversation stung.

The truth was, he was standing on foreign ground. Had this meeting taken place when he'd arrived at MonikerTech, he would've been wearing his armor of pretentious confidence, and he would've been armed with a few biting remarks to prove that he wasn't afraid to play with the big boys. But after the last few days, he couldn't muster the energy to pretend. The only thing he knew for sure was that everything he'd believed about himself and his ability to lead had slowly unraveled over the last few days.

Questions echoed in the back of his mind. Did he have enough time to rebuild a presentation from scratch? Board members were on their way, and they expected him to play the part of the competent communicator, worthy of the Reed name. Time had run out. Could he pull it off?

He started there, repeating almost verbatim the fears and questions that had just crossed his mind and punctuating his confession with artificial humor. "I hope you don't use this conversation as ammo to wrangle BeyondYou out of my hands." Daniel meant it. He knew he was taking a huge chance by being vulnerable, but there was no going back. He wondered whether Paul would be horrified. But he knew Lynda would be awestricken at first, and then utterly delighted.

He took a gulp of water, waiting for Michael's response, which took what seemed like an eternity. Daniel could almost hear him thinking, "Who are you? And what have you done with Daniel Reed?" Daniel resisted the temptation to fill the silence, so he sat back in the comfortable leather chair, determined to wait for Michael. He was glad he had declined the glass of wine so he could remember this conversation later as one he conducted in his right mind.

"So what's your question for me?" Michael sat back in his chair and looked squarely at Daniel.

Daniel looked past Michael's gaze in order to ponder his response. His cards were on the table, and his compulsion to generate a brilliant response had disappeared. "On Monday, when I arrived, Chris said you requested a meeting with me at the end of my stay. Why did you want to meet with me?"

Michael smiled, seemingly amused that Daniel turned his own question on him. "I wanted to see if the stories about you were true."

"Ah! The stories—that I lack the Reed rudder to steady the BeyondYou ship."

"No, not those stories. I don't put much weight on what media pundits put out there. They're wrong most of the time."

Daniel could have hugged Michael. "What stories then?"

"The ones I heard from your father." Daniel didn't say anything, but his body language must have suggested confusion, because Michael clarified. "He loved and admired you—but you probably already know that."

A knot formed in Daniel's throat. He hesitated, feeling like suddenly everything he'd been worrying about—the presentations, the board, the investor, the rumors—all of his fears were inconsequential. "You knew my father—personally?"

"He had tremendous influence in my personal and professional life." Michael paused as if savoring a fond memory. "I still remember the conversations we had the two times we played golf together for a fundraiser event."

"My father didn't play golf." As soon as he heard himself say those words, Daniel wondered if he even knew for sure.

Michael chuckled. "He didn't. Neither do I." In fact, we were terrible at it, so we ended up talking more than paying attention to our pitiful scores." Michael laughed. "It was all for a good cause."

Daniel hesitated. "What did he say about me?"

"That you were going to change the world one day."

Daniel put his hand over his glass as the waiter delivered the food and tried to refill Daniel's water glass. "Do you remember when that conversation took place?" Daniel took a deep breath, trying to keep his composure.

"Let me see," Michael stared at the deep red wine in his glass as he swirled it. "If I remember correctly, you had just turned down his offer to work for BeyondYou."

Daniel paused, suspecting that Michael knew much more about his relationship with his father than he was letting on. "We didn't exactly part on good terms. Did he mention that?"

"Yes, he sure did," Michael threw his head back and chuckled at the memory. "He said you inherited his sense of adventure, his entrepreneurial spirit—and your mother's tenacity—he might have said stubbornness."

Daniel wasn't amused. "Go on."

"He said you needed to find your own way—though he secretly knew one day you would be running BeyondYou."

"He said that?"

"Not with those exact words. Maybe I read between the lines. He did say that you didn't realize yet how truly special you were, and that when you discovered the Bridge Builder inside you, you would be unstoppable."

Daniel remained silent. He looked up at the ceiling, sensing that emotion was about to roll down his cheek. Then, in that same moment, he remembered the words his father had spoken all through his rebellious senior year of high school and through his proud college years. "Son, when you discover how special you are—and learn to build bridges—you will be unstoppable."

He remembered how he had never taken those words at face value, as a true reflection of how his father saw him. He'd interpreted them as a manipulative tactic to turn him into his father's clone.

And that, Daniel had determined, would never happen.

Michael must have read the struggle on his face because he allowed Daniel to sit in silence for as long as he needed. Daniel's mind was a haze of memories and images. He tried to formulate a question or comment, but nothing would come. Michael's words had effectively robbed him of all his concerns about Paul, the board, and the mysterious investor.

Daniel couldn't explain what was taking place inside him, but a weight was slowly lifting from his shoulders.

Daniel didn't know how long the two of them sat in silence, but it finally occurred to him that there was only one question he still felt an urgency to ask. "If one of your sons were in the position I'm in, what would you say to him?"

A paternal smile formed on Michael's face as he paused for a few seconds. Then he spoke.

"Daniel, you are not your father, but you are your father's son. Whether you decide to embrace or reject his legacy as a launch pad for your own is entirely up to you."

The words carried the force of a blow, and for a moment Michael froze. Then he slowly rose, took his jacket from where it hung on the back of the chair, and prepared to leave. "As for me, I can't wait to see what you'll choose to do, Daniel," he said as he squeezed Daniel's shoulder. "Like your father, I believe you *can* change the world. But the only opinion that really matters—the only question that remains is, do you?"

 **Bridge Builder Notes**

At the end of the day, what you believe about yourself is what really counts.

- Whose opinion of you matters most?
- What do you believe about yourself?

CHAPTER 31

PREPARING FOR BATTLE

Daniel arrived at his hotel room restless, even after walking along the harbor for almost two hours. He threw his jacket on the bed and glanced at the digital clock on the nightstand. He sighed. In less than twelve hours he would meet with Paul and the board. He wasn't close to being prepared, but surprisingly he wasn't anxious and didn't know exactly why.

He opened his computer to find Paul's email and half a dozen documents outlining BeyondYou's financial history, sales projections, product pipelines, and an elaborate report listing the major vulnerabilities they were facing as nervous investors rethought their partnership with BeyondYou. "We have the green light to use one of MonikerTech's war rooms for tomorrow's board meeting. Be ready for at least one curve ball. Morgan is coming."

Daniel laughed. Days ago, he would have been salivating over all the data and devising a strategy to showcase his ability and to put Morgan in his place. He might have even been fine-tuning his PowerPoint slides to dazzle investors with his knowledge. But now, the thought seemed ludicrous. He changed into a tee-shirt and gym shorts and walked to the window.

They chose me, for goodness sake. It was silly to think he could impress the board on a few days' notice. They knew what they were getting. *They came to me—whatever their initial motives were—they came to me.*

Michael's words echoed in his mind.

"I can't wait to see what you'll choose to do."

Daniel opened the window, but the unseasonably humid air increased the feeling of stuffiness. He turned on the air conditioning, then sat on the bed and opened his computer. He started to draft an email to Chris, hoping she'd agree to meet him at MonikerTech as early as possible, but he quickly deleted the draft. It was almost midnight, and there was no way she'd get it in time. He thought of calling Lynda, but he decided he didn't want to retell the whole story since so much had changed since the last time they'd spoken. Instead, he sent a quick text message: "Love you. Will call tomorrow."

He got up and paced the room. A surge of energy came over him as he realized everything he needed was already inside him—and inside the red binder he'd gotten from Tammy. He opened a bottle of water from the mini fridge and sat in the large leather chair near the window. He turned to page sixteen, knowing he would find the case study he should have read years ago. *In His Own Words: Daniel Reed Redefines "Beyond You" and Launches BeyondYou, Inc. Ahead of the Competition.*

"Unbelievable!" Daniel chastised himself over and over again as he read and reread the case study—which was more like a business memoir. Like a racehorse whose blinders had been finally removed, he could see how much he had missed.

He leaned his head back in the chair as he let the words he had read replay in his mind like a broken record.

I was such a fool.

Daniel was sleeping in the leather chair when the sound of the hotel phone woke him. He felt disoriented as the phone continued to ring and everything slowly came into focus. The red binder was still on his lap, the water bottle was full and untouched. He remembered reading the case study several times, then studying transcripts of BeyondYou employee interviews and meeting blueprints in the appendix. The last time he'd looked at the clock was five in the morning. He reached for the phone.

"Are you ok? I was about to send a search party for you." The voice belonged to Chris. "I've been calling your cell phone for the last hour."

"Yes, yes I'm fine." He grabbed his cell phone from the bed. The battery was dead. "What time is it?" He squinted at the clock.

"Almost ten. And guess who's just arrived?

"Rats!" The image of Paul surrounded by irritated board members flashed through his mind. He rotated his neck, working a knot that had formed at the top of his shoulders. "Tell them I'm on my way." Daniel was about to hang up, then . . . "Chris!"

"Yes, I'm still here."

"I have a favor to ask."

"Okay?"

"Would you join me at the board meeting—as my guest?"

Chris hesitated. "What do you have in mind?"

Daniel couldn't predict what the day would bring, but having sat through his fair share of board meetings, especially when a company faced uncertain change, he suspected he might be in for more than one round. "Let's just say I may need a coach in my corner after the first round is over."

"Say no more. Meet me in my office when you get in. We'll head to the war room together."

"Thank you, Chris. It means a lot."

Bridge Builder Notes

Sometimes the keys to what we want are closer than we think.

- What valuable information is available to you, but has remained unopened?
- What advice have you received in the past that is worth revisiting?

CHAPTER 32

SHOWTIME!

A sudden jolt, then the silver elevator doors wrenched apart. Daniel opened his eyes and discovered he was slumped in the corner as two eager faces peered down at him. Chris was there and Larry the friendly security guard. He could feel the air conditioning on his face. "I'm glad to see the air is back on," he mumbled, trying to reassure them. Larry gently lifted him with one arm behind his back while Daniel took Larry's other hand, still trying to assist in standing on his own two feet.

"Daniel, my goodness! Are you okay?" Chris reached down to help him, then guided him across the lobby to a white leather chair in the waiting area and put a cold bottle of water in his hand.

"I must've passed out." He chugged the water down. "How long was I in there?"

"About fifteen minutes," Larry said.

Daniel leaned his head back and closed his eyes—picking up his thoughts where he left off in the elevator, knowing that a mental review of his notes would come handy in a few minutes. His father's words came rushing in. "*A mentor once told me that it's almost as presumptuous to think you can do nothing as to think you can do everything.*" If ever he'd been in a position to think he could do nothing, this would be it. But he pushed the thought away.

He straightened himself up and took a deep breath. "Okay. Let's get this show on the road."

"Are you sure? I'm sure the board will understand if . . ."

He cut her off. "I'm fine. I feel better than I look."

"Good—because you look terrible," Chris chided with a grin as she handed him a second bottle of water, which he chugged in one long gulp.

"Are you sure you're ready?"

"As ready as I'll ever be." He tucked his shirt into his pants and smoothed his hair with his hands. "Besides, I have a Blueprint," he winked at her.

She gave him a look that screamed, "Where is it?"

He tapped his temple with his index finger. "It's all here. Trust me."

"Well, then, you are ready, Daniel Reed. Let's go." Chris handed him another bottle of water. "Just in case," she said as she led the way down the hallway.

"I had the strangest dream," he said between sips of water as he hurried behind her. "At least I think it was a dream."

"How strange?" She walked briskly.

"A sort of flashback—"

She cut him off. "Enough elevators for one day," she pointed to the escalators. As they approached the second floor, Daniel could see Paul and the rest of the group through the wall-to-ceiling glass window that overlooked the first floor of the atrium. "I'll tell you about it later," he said as he took a deep breath.

"Here we go. It's time to be a Bridge Builder, Daniel," Chris whispered.

"My apologies for being late," Daniel announced as he walked through the door, straightened his posture, and mustered all the executive presence he wished he felt. A shot of energy ran through his body. *It's about intention, not perfection,* he reminded himself.

"Shall we get started?" He sat his bottle at the head of the white rectangular table, across from Morgan, who stoically greeted him with a wave of his index finger, indicating he needed another minute to finish his phone call. Daniel took the opportunity to walk around the room and greet the other three board members.

He started to introduce them to Chris. To his surprise her reputation had preceded her, though he couldn't read whether that was a good or bad thing. One glance around the room told him that everyone seemed tense—even more than he was.

Jones, whom Daniel secretly referred to as Indiana Jones because his mannerisms reminded him of Harrison Ford's character in Daniel's favorite movie franchise, sipped coffee from a large ceramic mug. Dana was busy reading something on her phone. Susan just smiled.

Paul walked past Daniel and selected the black leather chair to his right. "Are you sick? You look terrible," he whispered as he leaned toward Daniel's shoulder.

"Thanks. I've heard." Daniel whispered back just as Morgan sat his cell phone down and reached for the triangular speakerphone on the table. He pressed a button and spoke.

"We're ready."

Daniel was glad he hadn't had time to imagine what this moment would be like, because he would have imagined it just the way it unfolded. Never in his life had he seen such a lack of affect in a group. There was no denying it—a big elephant was crowding the room.

"What's going on?" Daniel turned to Paul.

Morgan cut him off. "We need a quorum to vote. Some of the board members are joining remotely." He pushed his chair back from the table, leaned back, and crossed his legs. "Let's get started," he said.

Daniel remembered what Paul had said, about being ready for a curve ball.

"Daniel," Paul jumped in. "Before I turn the meeting to you, I think it's fair that you know what's going on here . . ."

Daniel was the one who cut him off this time. He could see what was going on, and this time it wasn't paranoia. They—or some of them—had come to their senses and realized what he had known all along, that it takes more than a Reed to refocus a company that is floundering without its leader.

But Morgan said they needed a vote, which meant that the board wasn't unanimous in their decision. He had a second chance to redeem himself, and he wasn't about to waste it.

"Paul, you don't have to say a word. I can see a coup written all over your faces. Someone here—and I mean Morgan—thinks it's time to withdraw your CEO offer." That's what Daniel wanted to say. But before the words had the chance to escape his lips, he rose to his feet and pushed his chair out of the way, slowly buying himself some time. He could see Chris from the corner of his eye. She looked like she was holding her breath.

"Paul, I'm sorry to interrupt you," Daniel finally said, "but if it's okay with all of you, I'd rather have the floor first. Paul looked around the table, as if checking for objections. Morgan shrugged his shoulders, as if saying, "It's fine by me." Indiana Jones, Smiley Susan, and Dana nodded as well.

Daniel leaned in and balanced himself on the table with his fingers, like a sprinter crouched at the starting blocks, waiting for the gun.

 **Bridge Builder Notes**

Teddy Roosevelt once said, "It is not the critic who counts; not the man who points out how the strong man stumbles, or where the doer of deeds could have done them better. The credit belongs to the man who is actually in the arena, whose face is marred by dust and sweat and blood; who strives valiantly . . ."

- When was the last time you were in the arena, striving valiantly?
- Whose criticism has counted—but needs to count no more?

CHAPTER 33

ELEPHANT IN THE ROOM

A s I look around the room, I believe a couple of questions are occupying your minds. The first—did we act hastily when we asked Daniel Reed, Jr., to step in as CEO?" Daniel couldn't be sure who was listening on the line, but from the looks on their faces, he was certain he had the attention of his audience in the room.

"The short answer—in my opinion—is YES." Sunny Susan suddenly lost her smile and turned to Indiana Jones, then to Paul. Daniel could instantly see who his allies were.

He straightened up and planted his feet firmly behind the head of the table as a sense of calm and confidence swept over him. "You *did* act hastily by asking me to step in as CEO when you did, thinking that simply installing another Reed would provide a quick Band-Aid for jittery investors." He paused. "Had I been a voting member of this board, I would have voted against me."

Susan sighed. She looked disappointed. Morgan uncrossed his legs and leaned forward as a grin slowly formed on his face.

"The second question you may be asking is—is there a better person to navigate BeyondYou through the rough waters and build a bridge to the investors we are courting right now?" Daniel paused for effect.

"You have my attention," Morgan blurted out, and Paul rolled his eyes.

Unaffected by the comment, Daniel continued. "The short answer to the second question is also *yes*—and that's exactly what I'd like to talk to you about for the next few minutes." Daniel took a sip from his water bottle, allowing himself the time to take a deep breath and slow down his heart rate.

"Bottom line, what BeyondYou needs right now is a Bridge Builder who can rally behind the culture that has made it the success that it is today." He paused again. "A Bridge Builder like my father. Someone who will look beyond self-interests and personal agendas. Someone who can look past the spin from the media and refocus the team. Someone who doesn't have all the answers, but is willing to ask the hard questions until the right answers emerge . . ."

Morgan took a deep sigh, refusing to hide his impatience. Daniel looked at his allies in the room.

"Someone whose failures and shortcomings have humbled him but not broken him. Someone who's willing to work tirelessly to nurture past, present, and future relationships—reminding them what made them want to partner with my father in the first place."

Daniel paused and looked around the room. The board members turned to look at each other as the seconds turned into an uncomfortable minute. And just as Morgan leaned in to speak, Daniel cut him off.

"The leader that BeyondYou needs today—wasn't me a week ago—and I believe we all can agree on that point." Everyone chuckled, except Morgan.

"But that isn't the man standing before you today, and . . ."

Morgan cut him off. "Great speech, Daniel. Unfortunately, we don't have time for lengthy speeches."

"I'm sorry, Morgan, but I personally would like to hear what Daniel has to say," Paul cut in.

"Paul," Susan offered as she shifted forward in her chair, "Morgan has a point. Let's not forget that our guest is on a time schedule."

Guest? What guest?

"I'd like to hear what Daniel has to say," a familiar voice came from the speaker phone.

Daniel glanced at Morgan. Morgan's face had turned red, and he looked like he was about to pop a blood vessel. "Thirty minutes," he spit out. "And not one second more."

Bridge Builder Notes

It takes guts to stand one's ground in the face of overt opposition.

- Whose opposition have you faced?
- Whose encouragement kept you going?

CHAPTER 34

SEEING ANEW

Daniel, you're right about one thing—we, as a board, acted impetuously and didn't properly vet you," said Susan firmly. "That is our fault—not yours."

Clearly, she had the gift of bringing civility back into the conversation, Daniel observed. Everyone, even Morgan, sat back and relaxed.

"I sense you know that today is about a critical decision for the future of BeyondYou. We need to either rectify our mistake or affirm our initial gut feeling that you are the right choice."

Paul crossed his arms as he spoke. "I believe I speak for everyone in this meeting—and do correct me if I'm wrong," he looked around the table to check in with everyone, "when I say that Daniel's assessment about the type of leader BeyondYou needs now is spot on."

"Yes. I agree." Voices echoed from the speakerphone. Daniel glanced around the room. Susan and Dana nodded. Morgan shrugged his shoulders with indifference.

Paul continued. "Daniel, maybe you can tell us what has made such a difference in your ability to lead between last week and now."

"That's fair," Daniel said, surprised by his sense of calm. He'd decided to use this opportunity as the formal interview he never got to have—his opportunity to clarify why he was in the best position to lead BeyondYou into a vibrant future. He looked in Chris's direction to find the affirming look of his mentor.

He was ready, and the realization had given him new confidence. He'd been preparing for decades—not just during the week he'd spent at MonikerTech, learning and observing a highly functioning Bridge Builder culture. Every conversation he'd had with Chris had reminded him of how much he had absorbed from his father over the years, despite his own arrogance and prideful resistance. Whether he liked it or not, he was born the son of the great Daniel Reed.

It was time to grow up. It was time to step into the legacy his father had left and to stop being resentful about being compared to a great man. In short, great leadership was not about him—it never had been. His father had taught him that.

In the moment of silence that followed, Daniel looked at the faces of his audience differently for the very first time. Standing before the men and women who had partnered with his father, Daniel felt a deep sense of awe and gratitude. These were the men and women who had been his father's partners and allies. They had helped shape BeyondYou into the company it was today, even if they were not part of the day-to-day operations of the company. Each and every one of them had brought something to the table—time, talent, or treasure. In fact, the more Daniel thought about it, the more he sensed there was something wrong with the picture before him.

As far as he knew, Morgan had been on BeyondYou's board from the very beginning. Why has he suddenly taken an adversarial position? What was Morgan thinking? How did he feel?

In a flash, the realization hit him. Daniel couldn't just stand in front of these great leaders and tell them what he had learned about building bridges—he had to find a way to show them, to show Morgan.

Daniel knew he was on the edge of what could be an insurmountable divide. Ready or not, it was time to attempt to build a bridge to his audience's hearts and minds.

I'm a Bridge Builder. I can do this!

Now, to believe it and do it.

He looked his board members in the eye and began.

 **Bridge Builder Notes**

Daniel sees his audience with fresh eyes for the first time, and his new perspective changes everything.

- What insights can you take away from Daniel's newfound perspective?
- What would realizing that your communication needs to be more about "showing" than "telling" cause you to do differently?

CHAPTER 35

SILENCE

I f I could narrow down everything I've learned and remembered from my father this week down to one key concept, it would be that my audience must always come first," said Daniel as he rose from his chair. "I could stand here and deliver a presentation to you—in fact, I have close to seventy PowerPoint slides ready to go." Paul, Susan, and Chris chuckled. "I could pretend that I know what you need to hear from me. But the truth is I don't."

Morgan cracked his neck as if he was trying his best to endure this meeting. Daniel kept moving forward, unaffected.

"So indulge me for a few minutes." Daniel walked toward the white board, uncapped a marker, and drew an enormous circle with the word *Why?* in the center.

"Why did you bring your time and resources to BeyondYou in the first place—why did you join my father, and why are you still here?"

Daniel's questions hung in the air.

"Silence is one of the most powerful communication tools a Bridge Builder owns. But even seasoned Bridge Builders must resist the temptation to answer their own questions." The voice of his father resonating in his memory surprised Daniel. He felt a sense of exhilaration as he realized how his new mindset was changing the way he conducted himself—from how he thought to how he listened to how he communicated.

Indiana Jones threw his head back and looked at the ceiling as if the answers to Daniel's questions were hanging from one of the air-conditioning ducts. Susan doodled on her legal pad, deep in thought. Dana turned to Paul and winced.

Silence. Not a sound stirred in the room or on the other side of the speakerphone. The seconds turned into minutes, but Daniel stood his ground.

Susan spoke first. "That's a great question. I don't know, Daniel. It's been a long time since I joined the BeyondYou team. All I remember is that Daniel—your father—had a knack for getting people onboard. His passion for what BeyondYou technology could do for the industry—for underprivileged groups—was contagious."

"I agree," Dana added. "I brought my contacts to BeyondYou because I trusted Daniel more than his technology. Don't get me wrong, the product and market share potential were a big part of my decision to join the team—but it all came down to one thing—relationship. That's what brought me to the table, and that's why I stayed."

"For me it was all about the money," Paul interjected.

"Sure, Paul." Morgan turned to him and rolled his eyes, cracking a smile for the first time. The room erupted in laughter. "You joined Daniel when he was still losing money—lots of money."

"Let's just say I could see Daniel was going places," Paul answered. "But seriously, I'm with Dana. For me, it was first about the relationship with Daniel and then about the product. Daniel was the type of person I wanted to be in business with, and I knew that his commitment to building relationships with others would pay off sooner or later. The rest is history."

"This is Roy," said a commanding voice from the speakerphone. "Until now, I didn't realize that relationship was a big reason why I joined Daniel. I've sat on the boards of many companies before, and I learned that no amount of money is worth partnering with someone I can't work with—someone who's a pain in the ass, pardon my French."

The room erupted into laughter. Morgan got up and stalked out of the room, letting the door slam behind him as the laughter faded again to silence.

 Bridge Builder Notes

Silence is one of the most powerful communication tools a Bridge Builder owns.

- When is silence most powerful?
- How often do you use silence as a powerful communication tool?

CHAPTER 36

EMPATHY

An awkward moment of silence followed. Daniel observed as Paul reached across the table and pointed the speakerphone toward himself, then spoke. "Let's take a fifteen-minute break. We'll be back online at the top of the hour." He muted the line.

"What just happened?" Daniel asked. Susan shrugged her shoulders. Paul winced. Dana lowered her head and stared at her crossed hands, avoiding eye contact with the rest of the group.

"Dana, do you know something we don't know?" asked Paul. "You know Morgan better than any of us."

Dana took a deep breath as if she were buying time.

"Dana, I know Morgan has been an integral part of BeyondYou for a long time. If my memory serves me right, he's brought over a quarter of a billion dollars of his own money to BeyondYou. If there's anything you can share that could help me understand why Morgan's taking such an adversarial position here today, I'd appreciate the insight."

Daniel sat down and looked at Chris, who nodded as if saying, "You're doing great."

Dana paused for what seemed an eternity. "Ok. Morgan will never say this—and probably will never forgive me for saying it—but he's still grieving Daniel's passing. Daniel was more than a business partner for Morgan. He told me once over drinks that Daniel came alongside him when he was at the lowest point of his life. He'd even considered suicide shortly after his wife left and took the kids with her. For a year, Daniel picked him up on Sunday mornings and took him to church with him. Then they'd go have lunch at that greasy spoon diner downtown." She chuckled. "Daniel was like a brother to Morgan. There was nothing Morgan wouldn't do for Daniel."

Confusion was written all over Paul and Susan's faces. They were obviously hearing this information for the first time, too.

A knot began to form in Daniel's throat.

"I might as well spill out the rest," Dana sighed. "Morgan resents you for turning your back on your father." She paused. "He thinks you broke his heart . . ."

The door opened abruptly, cutting her off. Everyone turned to look at Morgan, who walked stoically back to his chair, then glanced around the table with a puzzled look.

"We're on a fifteen-minute break," Paul interjected, explaining the awkward silence in the room. "I think we're ready to resume," he said as he unmuted the speakerphone.

Daniel felt every one's eyes on him as they waited for his next statement. But overwhelming feelings of empathy and sorrow over what Dana had shared had stripped any trace of pretense or scheme left in him. What he had feared most of his life was now his reality.

Daniel Reed, Jr., was facing his audience naked and without armor.

 **Bridge Builder Notes**

Empathy and vulnerability.

- What role should empathy have in your communication?
- Have you ever found yourself facing an audience "naked and without any armor"?

VULNERABILITY

D aniel reached for his chair and lowered himself into his seat. He leaned back, letting the silence hang in the air. His mind raced for a few seconds.

"This morning, when I was stuck in the elevator I remembered something that happened a long time ago, and now I feel like I need to share it with you before we go any further.

"I had just finished my junior year of high school. I was nursing a foot injury from stepping on a broken bottle while running late at night. I should've stayed off my feet, getting myself ready for track season, but sitting around the house was killing me. So against my mother's advice and my better judgment, I rode my bike to the local feed mill and asked if there were any openings for summer jobs.

"The foreman gave a me a familiar look, the same look I got from the football coach when I asked if I could join the team. Looking at my 120-pound frame, the foreman chuckled and said, 'Sure, I've got just the job for you.'

"I'd always thought that working at the mill would be a blast. I pictured myself driving forklifts from the tractor-trailers on the loading docks. I also thought it would be cool to operate the grain-loading systems. One of my friends who had worked there before told me all about mixing the grain according to a prescribed formula of vitamins and minerals.

"But the foreman led me straight to a warehouse area in the middle of the plant and explained I'd be working 'The Wheel.' There was in fact a large wheel, flat on its side, that constantly turned. A conveyer belt dropped feed onto the wheel. The guy I was relieving stood on a platform next to the wheel, picked up 100-pound bags of feed off the wheel, and dropped them onto a skid about three feet below the platform.

"Now, the bags couldn't just be thrown carelessly onto the skid. They had to be positioned just right. Four bags to a row piled four rows high—sixteen bags per skid.

"If they weren't positioned just right, they'd fall off the skid and the forklift driver would let you know, in no uncertain terms, that it better not happen again.

"Now picture this. I weighed 120 pounds soaking wet. The feedbags weighed 100 pounds. The bags were awkward to grab and maneuver. Eight hours a day for two days I loaded skids with feedbags. I went home exhausted and with my foot swollen—but I didn't want to hear my mother say, 'I told you so,' so I got up early in the morning ready to load more skids with bags of grain.

"On my third day at the wheel, the foreman hired a big brawny dude, whose neck was as big as both of my thighs put together. He was supposed to take my place at the wheel. Boy, if I could have jumped for joy, I would have. My savior had come to deliver me. Or so I thought.

"I arrived the next day, hoping my next assignment would involve driving a forklift. But no such luck. As it turned out, the big dude never came back.

"'What happened?' I asked the foreman when he told me I was back on the wheel.

"He said, 'I have been here a long time, and I can tell you that it's not the size of the dog in the fight, but the size of the fight in the dog.' Then he walked off."

Daniel paused. A pin drop could be heard in the room. "So now I'm on my fourth day at the wheel and working the evening shift. I'm physically and mentally spent." Daniel got up from his chair and began to move around as if he were back in that old feed mill. "I toss the first bag on the skid, but it's not aligned just right. I jump off the platform to reposition it. By the time I get back on the platform, five or six bags are on the wheel. In a few minutes, bags are coming off the conveyor belt and falling off the wheel. Man! Catching up seems impossible. Now there are ten bags of feed on the wheel and about thirty on the ground, and more of them are falling.

"It's at that moment that I see the red button on the wall, the button no one is supposed to push because all production comes to a stop. *Never press the red button.* That was the unspoken rule. I look all around me, and everyone seems to be gone. No forklifts. No one walking around, just me and a sea of feedbags where they aren't supposed to be.

"In a panic, I pressed the red button. I began to pick up the 100-pound bags, one by one.

"I wanted to cry. I was tired and at my wits end. All I wanted to do was to throw in the towel and go home.

"Then my father's voice started ringing in my head. 'You are Daniel Reed—you are my son—and you can do this!'

"And just like that, a surge of energy came over me. I started picking up the bags with renewed strength. One by one, I piled them up on the skids. I pressed the red button to restart production and finished another day at the wheel with my head held high.

"Next day was Friday. I got the rhythm of the job down, and I finished up the day. As I headed out the door, the foreman stopped me and said, 'Hey, Reed—next week you're on forklift duty.' And for the rest of the summer, I drove the forklift and ran the bulk grain-mixing machine.

"Later I found out that the wheel was a test. The size of a man didn't matter—just his resolve to succeed and to push the limits of his work ethic."

Daniel paused, letting the flow of emotion that had come over him subside. Then he looked into the eyes of his father's business partners and his loyal friends. "I learned determination and work ethic from my father. He taught me how to work hard. He taught me never to quit. He taught me to be proud to be his son . . . I am Daniel Reed—my father's son. But for far too long, I forgot who I was. Until this week."

Daniel looked at Morgan across the conference table. "This week I also remembered that no man or woman can succeed alone. That's what my father tried to teach me until the day he died." Daniel reached into his pocket and pulled out the folded, worn out piece of paper he had read dozens of times. He unfolded it and put it on the table.

"You are here to decide whether I can be the Bridge Builder BeyondYou needs at the helm. But even if you affirm your earlier decision, even if you allow me to come home and take my father's place—I have learned that I can only succeed if you stand with me like you stood with him—without reservation, no holds barred."

Daniel paused again and took a deep breath. "My father trusted you, and that's enough for me. If you allow me to take the wheel of BeyondYou, I will work with the resolve and work ethic of the young man in the mill. I will work tirelessly to become the Bridge Builder BeyondYou needs—with *your* help."

Slowly, Daniel got up from his chair and stood tall in the silence as his audience looked at him. "Thank you for giving me the opportunity to tell you who I am. I believe you now have a vote to discuss."

With those words lingering in the air, Daniel turned and exited the conference room.

Bridge Builder Notes

Story is possibly the most disarming communication tool at your disposal.

- Can you think of a particular story or stories in your life that influenced who you are and how you lead?
- Have you ever shared them with someone else?
- What was the outcome?

CHAPTER 38

LEADING AUTHENTICALLY

D aniel Reed—a man who learned what it means to work at the local feed mill," Chris chided as she closed the door of her office behind Daniel. "I wouldn't have guessed it in a million years. I'll refrain from embarrassing you and gushing like a mother whose baby just made her proud by taking his first steps all by himself."

Daniel grinned as he let himself fall into one of the leather chairs. He felt like he had just finished running a marathon.

"And I wouldn't have guessed that Michael Thompson was the mysterious investor who would have saved BeyondYou had Morgan gone rogue."

Chris sat back in the chair across from him and chuckled. "When did you figure it out?"

"I recognized his voice on the speaker phone." Daniel reached for a fresh bottle of water that sat on the coffee table. "I had a hunch last night. After I *finally* read BeyondYou's case study and learned that my father was MonikerTech's first angel investor—and the friend Michael referred to in his keynote—the friend who showed him a different way."

Daniel took a gulp of water. "Everything began to make sense. Why Michael allowed me to steal you for a week. Why he's let me look under the MonikerTech hood." He sighed. "Why he's put up with my childish arrogance."

Daniel leaned his head back. He closed his eyes as the silence hung in the air. "Well, it's all up to the board now."

"We should know their decision soon. I told Paul to text me when they were ready for you."

Neither of them spoke for several minutes, until Daniel opened his eyes. Chris broke the silence. "So the wheel story. That's the dream—the flashback you had in the elevator?"

"Part of it." He grinned.

"Well, are you going to tell me the rest or not?"

Daniel straightened up. "I told the same story to Lynda the day after she got engaged to her fancy pants lawyer. It all came back to me in the elevator."

"Let's hear it."

"She'd just moved back to Los Angeles. I was still in the Bay Area, finishing business school. I was up to my eyeballs with final projects and exams, but I couldn't focus. I knew she was the one for me, but she never took me that seriously. I thought we had something special, but she thought I was 'a man-child with a distorted view of the real world.' Not her exact words, but that's pretty much what she meant."

"So was she right?"

"Only the distorted view of the world part." He winked. "I always thought she'd come around and see how wrong she was about the man-child thing. Sooner or later she'd come to her senses, or so I thought."

"But she got engaged to her fancy lawyer anyway."

"Friday night, the week before finals and all my deadlines, that's when I found out. I couldn't study. I couldn't focus. So I jumped in my car and drove to Los Angeles."

"Wow!"

"Six hours on the road, that's how long I had to prepare my presentation." Chris chuckled. "After a couple of hours on the road, I began to see things from her perspective. And the longer I thought about it, the more I realized why she thought I was out of her league."

"Really!"

"Daniel Reed, the man-child. She assumed, like most people, that because I was Daniel Reed, everything had been handed to me. I was used to being treated like a spoiled brat, riding on my father's coattail." He paused and took a sip of water. "Of course that wasn't true, and anyone who knew my dad knew better."

Daniel paused as scenes from the past flickered through his mind. "Anyway, I never bothered to tell her the truth, because by the time we met I'd already developed a sizable chip on my shoulder about all things Reed. What I didn't realize was that I'd taught myself to ignore my wisest counselors and shut out people who could be my greatest assets. I had no idea how negatively my mindset would influence our marriage." Daniel shook his head. So many bridges to repair—to begin building to Lynda's heart.

He continued. "Lynda, on the other hand, was always the real deal. She wasn't ashamed of her humble beginnings and never let her sizable accomplishments define her. She always knew who she was. You probably read her story."

"Yes, I did. She ran in the Olympics. Won gold. Then she upset the sports world by retiring and putting her endorsement money into her non-profit to help victims of sex trafficking."

"That's my Lynda."

"So what happened when you got to LA?"

"I arrived at her mother's house, where she was staying. It was four in the morning, and I thought about knocking, but I knew I'd look like a stalker. So I drove to a nearby hotel and checked into a room—mainly so I could clean up and put on the suit I'd thrown in the back seat before leaving."

Daniel leaned forward, reliving the moment all over again. He knew he was grinning like a schoolboy and didn't care. "I showed up at her door by eight, wearing my best blue suit—looking like a respectable almost MBA graduate, who's already received a couple of respectable job offers. I told her that I happened to be in the neighborhood." Daniel laughed. "How stupid must that have sounded?

"Long story short, I convinced her to go out for a drive. I told her that the attorney was all wrong for her and—sort of proposed . . ."

She cut him off. "Sort of proposed?"

"What can I say? I'd been up for twenty-four hours."

"Unbelievable!"

"Anyway, I can see that I'm not making a dent in her perception of me. I'm at the end of my rope, so out of nowhere, I tell her the wheel story you heard today—and spill my guts." He paused and shook his head.

"This is the part I want to hear."

"I told her that I wasn't the spoiled and entitled guy everyone thought I was. I said something like, 'It's true my father has given me a lot, but it's not what everyone thinks—he's given me determination, work ethic, autonomy to follow my dreams and make my own mistakes, and a healthy dose of truth that reminds me—now and again—I have every reason in the world to be proud to be the son of Daniel Reed.' Something like that."

"That's it?"

"I might have said that if I were so lucky to have her by my side, I could change the world. "

Chris leaned in. "Daniel, that's amazing! What did she say?"

"Nothing. I think I rendered her speechless. As you know, I'm not a big fan of touchy-feely stuff, so I was totally out of character. I think I must have disarmed her in a crazy sort of way."

"Then what?"

"Everything after that is kind of a blur. I'm sure I embarrassed myself even more. She just listened. We walked around the Santa Monica Pier.

I took her back to her place, and I left her with a kiss on the cheek, then I said good-bye. I got in my car and drove back home—six excruciating hours, fighting a vulnerability hangover."

"You've got to be kidding me!"

"Well, what did you expect? A chick flick ending?"

"So then what?"

"At the end of finals week, she called me and said she was going to be in the Bay Area and would love to come to my graduation. After the ceremony, she told me she broke it off with the lawyer. A month later we were engaged. The rest is history."

"What do you mean the rest is history? What about the wheel story? Did she ever mention it? Did she say how it impacted her decision to break the engagement?"

Daniel smiled. "Not right away. Soon after we were married, she told me that the wheel story—and my willingness to show her the real me—gave her hope." He paused and beamed, like someone savoring a rare and exquisite treat. "She said that kissing her cheek, like a perfect gentleman, melted her heart and gave her a glimpse of the kind of man I was capable of becoming." He smiled. "She might have said something like, 'I can work with a guy like that.'"

"That's a great story, Daniel! You don't even realize it, but you've just shared a story that belongs in your Bridge Builder Manifesto!"

"What in the world is a Bridge Builder Manifesto?"

"Bridge Builders who lead authentically have a Bridge Builder Manifesto—a growing collection of defining stories that capture experiences so authentic, so undeniable, that they have the power to transform—both the person who experienced them and those who hear the stories. The Manifesto, in essence, becomes the story about what made you who you are, your character, your potential, and your most authentic influence."

Daniel leaned back in the chair. "Can you elaborate?"

"Do you know what a plumb line is?"

"A plum line? A line with a plum attached to it?"

She cracked up. "Close. P-l-u-m-b. Plumb line. A plumb line is a cord weighted with lead. It's used in building to determine whether vertical structures are perfectly vertical—in other words, perfectly true."

Daniel was still laughing. "Go on."

"Your Bridge Builder Manifesto is a plumb line. It shows what it looks like to be true to yourself—and why being completely true to who you are is the only way to garner the trust and loyalty of those you want to reach. Your Bridge Builder Manifesto helps you determine your most authentic and rewarding characteristics of leadership and influence."

She paused, giving Daniel time to let her words sink in.

"You mean that the Bridge Builder Manifesto reveals the source of my influence and shows it in action. Is that it?" He leaned forward.

"You got it!"

"Ironic isn't it? For years I resented my father and being compared to him. I wanted to be my own man. I wanted to prove that I could do everything on my own. Yet, his fingerprints have always been on everything I've ever accomplished—and everything I was willing to work hard to get." Daniel paused and smiled. This time, it felt like the smile of a proud son. "Well, if the board votes in my favor today, I'll have one more story for my Manifesto. And the hero of the story will once again be . . . Dad."

Chris smiled—the look of a proud teacher, pleased to see her star student connect all the dots by himself. Daniel wondered if she could see the man Lynda had envisioned years earlier—and the son Daniel Reed, Sr., raised—being transformed right before her eyes.

He interrupted her reverie. "So everyone has a Bridge Builder Manifesto?"

"Everyone has stories to create a Bridge Builder Manifesto—the Manifesto itself is the result of intentional reflection and evaluation of those stories and their significance when they drive forward action. The Manifesto is the story behind the data, so to speak."

"So there's more I can still learn from you, then," he winked with a hint of anticipation.

"That's right. You're not getting rid of me just yet." She smiled back.

"So what do you think? Do I have a chance? With the board, I mean."

"More than that. Today, at the board meeting, you stepped in front of everyone as a leader, like you did at the mill and when you spoke to Lynda—unashamed to say, 'This is who I am and this is how I lead.' You showed them who you are—the source of your leadership and what motivates you.

"You risked it all for the sake of genuine relationship and the right to lead authentically. You invited each and every one of those men and women both to join you and follow you without compromising who you are—that's what leading like a Bridge Builder is all about. You have everything to gain. If the board members say 'yes'—they will be welcoming you as an authentic leader, not as their pawn."

"But there are no guarantees they'll say yes."

"Only the guarantee that they chose to follow an authentic Bridge Builder before—and that they're desperately looking to follow an authentic Bridge Builder again."

Standing against the backdrop of blue skies and a view of the Coronado Bridge, Daniel caught a reflection of himself in the glass. For some unknown reason, he looked taller than when he arrived at the beginning of the week. His posture was different. A new energy radiated from within. Chris had noticed it and commented on it when he first arrived at her office that morning: "The unmistakable strength that comes from those who know exactly what they want and who they are—and neither their desires, nor their true identity are compromised by the other."

Daniel reached into his pocket and pulled out the worn out letter he'd carried all week long and read and re-read dozens of times. He opened it and scanned it again, although he already knew every word by heart. He smiled, as he found words that stood out anew: ". . . Not money. Not power. Not the greatest product. Not shrewd business savvy. Not even talent, timing, or intelligence fueled my success. *People who were willing to join and follow my leadership* have always been the fuel." The power of his father's words struck him.

He looked up at Chris. She smiled, then turned to read a text message on her phone. "The board has reached a decision. They're ready for you."

Daniel folded the letter and pressed the creases like a curator handling a priceless document. He looked up and met her gaze. No words were needed. Daniel's serene expression told the story. Both of them sensed that the outcome would be favorable—but also knew it was inconsequential to the bigger picture. Daniel had accepted his father's gift—and saw that it was precious beyond words. And even more precious was knowing that Lynda waited for him at home and that he'd rediscovered the way to build a bridge to her heart.

Daniel looked out at the Coronado Bridge one last time and took a deep, renewing breath. Then he turned toward his father's mentor—and his own.

"No matter what happens in the next few minutes, I'm going home today—and it's going to be a great day. Thank you, Chris. No matter what the board decides, you've taught me to be a Bridge Builder, although you will always be *The* Bridge Builder to me. Because of you, I'm a changed man with a new vision for people—not just my board or BeyondYou, but my wife and everyone I meet.

"The board will make a decision today, but it won't be about winning or losing. I've already won, because I have finally accepted my father's gift. And I'll never see myself and the people in my world the same way again."

Bridge Builder Notes

Leading authentically.

- What does leading authentically mean for you?
- Do you know anyone who possesses "the unmistakable strength that comes from those who know exactly what they want and who they are—and neither their desires, nor their true identity are compromised by the other"?
- What characteristics do you share with them?
- Is there a gift you haven't been willing to accept?

The End
(of the story, not the book)

PART II

THE BRIDGE BUILDER APPROACH

"As a business leader, you have several constituencies: employees, bosses, boards of directors and advisors, customers, partners, investors, and so on. It helps to have a playbook with notes on how to communicate most effectively in each of these scenarios."
—**Eric Schmidt** & **Jonathan Rosenberg**, *How Google Works*

CHAPTER 39

HIGH-LEVEL OVERVIEW

D o you remember the premise for this book? Let me repeat it, so you don't have to run back to the introduction: You already know how to be a Bridge Builder—although you may not realize it. Like most people, you've probably forgotten. But you've successfully built bridges before. Intention, not perfection, helped you achieve what you wanted. And intention, not perfection, will help you achieve what you want in the future.

The Bridge Builder Approach is a proven communication and strategic leadership method for building bridges to the hearts and minds of your audiences. It encompasses proven principles, best practices, and tools that will help you become a more influential communicator and leader.

- **Bridge Builder Principles** are best communication and leadership practices or habits that set Bridge Builders apart: Think like a Bridge Builder, Listen Like a Bridge Builder, Act

Like a Bridge Builder, Talk Like a Bridge Builder, and Lead Like a Bridge Builder. Each of these principles stands on three foundational attitudes—empathy, authenticity, and respect.

- **SUPERB Communication Tools** help you craft persuasive communication that connects with the hearts and minds of your target audiences: Story, Usefulness, Passion, Empathy, Reliability, and Brevity. The online **Superb Assessment** will help you identify areas of strength and opportunities for development.

- **Bridge Builder Manifesto** is your personal leadership plumb line. It contains selected and refined stories that align you to your most authentic and rewarding Bridge Builder leadership.

- **Blueprints** are shortcuts to effective, day-to-day communication. You'll find some included in this book and many more on the Book Resource Website: LeadersBuildBridges.com.

Each best practice and tool complements one another, as part of a comprehensive strategy, and also stands on its own.

Individuals and organizations can adopt principles and tools gradually, as part of a linear development strategy, as illustrated below, or as an ongoing process, as illustrated in the **Principles** sections that follow and the **Visual Action Plan** described in the last chapter.

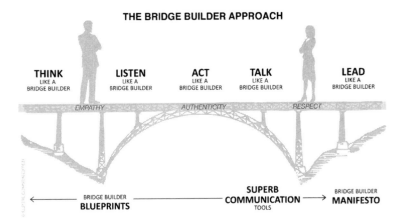

THE BRIDGE BUILDER APPROACH

THINK	LISTEN	ACT	TALK	LEAD
LIKE A	LIKE A	LIKE A	LIKE A	LIKE A
BRIDGE BUILDER	BRIDGE BUILDER	BRIDGE BUILDER	BRIDGE BUILDER	BRIDGE BUILDER

EMPATHY   AUTHENTICITY   RESPECT

←———— BRIDGE BUILDER **BLUEPRINTS** ————   **SUPERB COMMUNICATION** TOOLS ———→   BRIDGE BUILDER **MANIFESTO**

When the Bridge Builder Approach becomes part of your communication and leadership DNA—and the DNA of your organization's culture—the results will amaze you.

Can you imagine what can happen when you and your team begin to think, listen, act, talk, and lead like Bridge Builders? Can you imagine the relationships you'll build with those you want to reach with your message?

But I'm getting ahead of myself. Let's dive deeper, and you be the judge.

CHAPTER 40

THE BRIDGE BUILDER
PRINCIPLES

"There are three constants in life: change, choice, and principles."
—Stephen Covey

Principle 1: Think Like a Bridge Builder

It's no surprise that world-class athletes invest as much time in building and maintaining their mental capacity as in refining the hard skills of their sport—perhaps even more. Most of them will tell you that psychology—the way you think about yourself, your ability, and your potential—is more important than raw talent or even the work itself.

The same principle is true for world-class communicators.

In the parable, Daniel initially fights against taking the first step toward solving his problems—thinking like a Bridge Builder. When he changes his attitude, he begins to see what other Bridge Builders around him have learned: The things we care about are bridges— if communicated well—to the hearts of others who care about the same things.

This principle is true for you. Your sales are built on your ability to build a bridge to a customer who cares about your product. Gaining a bigger platform is built on your ability to relate to an audience who cares about your message. Funding success is built on nurturing investors who believe in the viability of your ideas and your ability to execute them. Getting a promotion or a raise is built on your ability to convince your boss that you're an invaluable asset to your organization.

As you build bridges to your audience, you earn influence, trust, and permission to lead.

Learning to think like a Bridge Builder is not only the first, but also the most crucial of all five principles. In fact, it is foundational to the Bridge Builder Approach.

In *The Power of Habit: Why We do What We Do in Life and Business*, Charles Duhigg talks about keystone habits, the type of habits that can trigger widespread change."[1] Thinking like a Bridge Builder—*believing* that your purpose as a communicator and as a leader is to build bridges to others—is a keystone habit that will trigger the other four.

Thinking like a Bridge Builder means adopting a Bridge Builder Identity, the most consuming part of the Bridge Builder Approach. Daniel illustrates how difficult it can be to walk away from old habits and preconceived ideas that keep us from wanting to become Bridge Builders.

When the shift takes place, we see the world from a new point of view—and *you* will see the world and the people around you from a new perspective. New communication habits replace old priorities. Your audience—your clients, your allies—will become your priority. Your approach to preparing a presentation, leading a meeting, engaging in a conversation, or working through a confrontation will begin with the person on the receiving side of your conversation. No more rehearsed scripts. No more predictable PowerPoint presentations. No more sermons. No more preparation based on what's convenient for you or what you'd like to say.

Your goal will be to build bridges to your audience—and not just their minds, but their hearts as well.

A caveat
Building bridges starts with one person who wants to do just that—build a bridge in order to create true connection. But from time to time, you'll find people who won't be moved—no matter how intentional you are. In the parable, we see that CT is what Tammy calls a "communication terrorist." She is never going to change. Individuals who burn bridges as a hobby or for their own private reasons choose to close their hearts and minds to others, regardless of how hard you may try to build a bridge. These individuals can poison your teams, your relationships, and your organizations if you give them space for negative influence. Intention, in this case, means simply this: never sacrifice your attitude or your culture (as a leader) over those who will fight to the death for their limitations. If people argue for their limitations, let them keep them.

Bridge Builder Notes

The skill of thinking like a Bridge Builder, alone, can revolutionize your influence.

* On a scale from 1 to Einstein, how much of the time do you think like a Bridge Builder, as described in this section?
* How can you tell whether someone thinks like a Bridge Builder?

Blueprint: Thinking Like a Bridge Builder.

> *"If you believe you can change—*
> *if you make it a habit—the change becomes real."*
> —**Charles Duhigg**, *The Power of Habit*

Thinking differently about yourself starts with changing the way you talk about yourself.

Say it. *I'm a Bridge Builder.* You may not feel like a Bridge Builder yet, but you can start with what I call "truth in advance."

I'm a Bridge Builder. As you say the words, you'll begin to think differently. You'll be more inclined to identify barriers and overcome them, not erect them. Your goal will be to understand first, before making yourself understood.

I'm a Bridge Builder. Those words alone will keep you from jumping to conclusions, gossip, and emotional diatribes. You'll begin to choose different words and approaches to convey what you want to say.

I'm a Bridge Builder. When the words turn into an identity, you will care more about your audience than about what you want. Ironically, you'll be able to get more of what you want because your audience will care more about you.

Thinking like a Bridge Builder is the hardest shift a communicator makes on the journey to becoming a Bridge Builder—but you can begin now. Start by stating it: *I'm a Bridge Builder.*

Remember, becoming a Bridge Builder is a matter of intention, not perfection—choosing to communicate differently. Telling yourself *I'm a Bridge Builder* every day is your first intentional step to becoming one.

In the parable, we see Michael taking drastic measures to ensure that every MonikerTech employee remembers to think like a Bridge Builder. In other words, he invests in building their identity as Bridge Builders—whether it's through the "I'm a Bridge Builder" wristbands everyone wears or through the extravagant campus design. Thinking like a Bridge Builder takes effort and constant reinforcement.

How will you remember to think like a Bridge Builder?

Be creative. Be intentional.

Blueprint: Connecting with Your Audience

Nancy Duarte helps companies design presentation stories. She teaches that the audience—not the presenter—is **the hero**. She gets that "the people you're addressing will determine whether your idea spreads or dies, simply by embracing or rejecting it."[2] I couldn't agree more. Bridge Builders get to know their audiences by asking these questions.

- Who is my audience?
- What is their background?
- What do they care about?
- What keeps them up at night?
- What do they already know about my topic?
- What do they need to know?
- What don't they need to now—right now?
- What do we share in common?
- What might be their objections to my message?
- How do they prefer to receive information?
- Why should they care about my message?

Once you gather information about your audience, ask some of these questions:

- How does my message solve a problem for my audience?
- How do I get them unstuck?
- How can I give them an *aha* moment?
- How can I help them discover a shortcut?
- How can I inspire them to change the world?
- Remember, building bridges is not about you—it's about the heroes before you.

Principle 2: Listen Like a Bridge Builder

My business partner recently facilitated a communication activity in which participants were asked to pair up. One was asked to first assume the role of listener while the other shared, based on a couple of initial questions. The "listener" was first instructed to ask a personal question in order to better understand what his or her communication partner cared deeply about. Then, he or she had to be attentive and not to interrupt until the person sharing was completely finished.

Halfway through the activity, a woman excused herself and walked out of the room. Later, she shared privately that it was out of character for her to be so emotional—especially in public. "I can't remember the last time someone *really* listened," she said.

Listening is one of the most neglected aspects of communication—whether we're at home or at work. Listening isn't easy, because it requires "concentration"—emptying one's cup. Jerry Weissman illustrates that principle with this story:

A Japanese Zen master received a university professor who came to inquire about Zen. The Zen master knew from the start of the conversation that the professor wasn't as interested in learning about Zen as he was in impressing the master with his own opinions and knowledge. The master listened patiently and finally suggested that they have tea. The master poured his visitor's cup full and then kept pouring.

The professor watched the cup overflowing until he could no longer restrain himself. "The cup is overfull, no more will go in!"

"Like this cup," the master said, "you are full of your own opinions and speculations. How can I show you Zen unless you first empty your cup?"

> Listening in order to have a chance to respond.
> Listening to insert your own story.
> Listening only to hear what your want to hear.
> Listening to catch something you can later use against the person sharing.
> Listening with contempt.

These forms of listening are **not** the trademarks of a Bridge Builder—they, however, are clues that the "listener" isn't showing up to the conversation with an empty cup.

Building your listening skills is one of the greatest investments you will make as a Bridge Builder, especially if you want to build trust with your team. Patrick Lencioni puts it best: "It's as simple as this. When people don't unload their opinions and feel like they've been listened to, they won't really get on board."[3]

Bottom line, communicators who listen like Bridge Builders immediately stand out from the crowd, because so few people know how to listen.

How Do Bridge Builders Listen?

The traditional Chinese symbol for listening embodies all the characteristics Bridge Builders value. Listening means using not just the ears, but also the eyes, the mind, and the heart—with undivided attention and the respect given to a king. Listening, then, communicates an act of empathy and respect.

Chinese Character for Listening

Ears · Eyes · Focus · King · Heart

Bridge Builders listen to understand.

Listening to understand means listening with your mind. It means withholding judgment. Anticipating positive intentions. Putting agendas aside. Not jumping in, trying to solve a perceived problem. Bridge Builders seek to understand before being understood. Before they proceed, they clarify: "What I hear you saying is . . . Did I understand you correctly?"

Bridge Builders listen with an open heart.

Listening with an open heart is called *empathetic listening*. We put ourselves in the shoes of the other person and try to see from their vantage point—not ours. We give the other person permission to be authentic without jumping to conclusions, without taking things personally, and without penalizing them for how they feel or express themselves. Bridge Builders pay attention to the emotion behind the words and are willing to withhold a response until they have a clear perspective.

Bridge Builders listen to learn something new.
No person is the exclusive repository of knowledge and wisdom. When we listen to learn, we approach people assuming that we *will learn* something from them and don't need to offer a solution, make a judgment call, give advice, or have the last word.

Bridge Builders listen with their ears and their eyes.
Bridge Builders know they can't multitask, so they put away distractions. They put away the phone. They close the computer. They ignore the noise around them. They honor their audience with their ears and their eyes.

 Bridge Builder Notes

Listening like a Bridge Builder is probably the most neglected principle.

- When was the last time you felt truly heard? What was that like?
- Listening like a Bridge Builder is an act of respect. What roles do authenticity, vulnerability, and respect play in this principle?

Blueprint: Listening Like a Bridge Builder

- Show up with an "empty cup."
- Be fully present: Put away the phone.

- Listen with your eyes: Make eye contact, but don't be creepy about it. Natural eye contact is not a staring contest.
- Listen with your body: Lean in, nod, and affirm.
- Listen with your heart: Withhold judgment. Assume positive intentions.
- Convey empathy: Offer neutral but authentic acknowledgment to indicate you are present (Really! Wow! Mmm . . . Oh my!).
- Paraphrase or clarify when you don't understand: "I'm not sure what you mean by that." "What I hear you saying is . . ." "Help me understand . . ."
- Embrace silence: Silence can be one of the most powerful elements of a conversation, opening doors to vulnerability and intimacy.
- Resist the temptation to hijack the conversation: Avoid steering the conversation with your own story, advice, or leading questions.

Principle 3: Act Like a Bridge Builder

A few months ago, a good friend and colleague, with whom I had collaborated on a mutually beneficial project, called me in the middle of the day. I could sense that something was bothering her. After brief chitchat, she confronted me on a choice I made that indirectly affected the result of our collaboration. She was angry and hurt, feeling I had acted selfishly and perhaps even unethically. Her emotions poured out with every word she shared, triggering my fight or flight instincts.

I wanted to defend myself and began to do so, but quickly forced myself to listen and let her finish without interrupting. The more she spoke, the more I felt the need to justify myself. I wanted to defend my actions and explain that she was overreacting and that what she was describing was not a character issue as she thought. But the more I listened, the more I realized that I needed to put myself in her place and see the situation from her perspective. The conversation was not about my perspective—at least not at that point.

I continued to listen quietly. I tried to see the situation from her perspective as she poured her heart out. Her chastising words cut me deeply, because being a person of character means a great deal to me. And according to the letter of the law, the incident she was describing would be a nonissue.

But I could not deny that I had undermined our relationship, because I had not taken into consideration how my choices told a different story from her perspective. There was so much I wanted to say, but I couldn't trust myself to speak because of the overwhelming emotions I was feeling.

I apologized for hurting her, and I promised that I would reflect further on what she had shared. We concluded our conversation, agreeing to reconnect in person at a later time.

When I hung up, I was overcome with emotion. I couldn't believe that this could happen between us after all we'd gone through as friends and collaborators.

But time and distance are often the corrective glasses that can help bring clarity to our perspective. I was grateful that travel commitments and the holiday season kept us from connecting until a couple of months later. Distance and time allowed me to pray and to review our conversation without emotion and from a variety of vantage points. In the process, three fresh perspectives emerged.

First, I saw why my actions came across as insensitive and even unethical. I became aware of a threatening blind spot common to type A individuals, who tend to gravitate to tasks and speed of execution, often without considering how others will be affected. Left unchecked, this blind spot slowly could have transformed me into a person I didn't want to become.

Second, I saw how blessed I was to have a friend who was willing to confront me and point out this blind spot—with authenticity—sharing exactly how my actions made her feel. I realized that she could have kept her resentment to herself, which would have eventually driven a permanent wedge between us. I was grateful she'd chosen to take a chance and call me.

Third, I saw that, although I was grateful for her confrontation, I also was deeply hurt by the fact that she had not given me the benefit of the doubt based on our history and my past contributions to our relationship. At least that's how I perceived her interpretation of events. I, too, had a choice to make. Would I resent her or would I trust that she'd want to consider my perspective?

I decided to lean in with trust, hoping she would welcome my sincerity as much as I welcomed hers.

However, I had already decided I would go to her without expectations. Whether she validated my feelings or not, I was determined not to let the outcome get in the way of our relationship.

I approached her and offered my perspective. She listened and acknowledged what I said and how I felt. I didn't know then whether she fully understood my perspective, but we both agreed that over time our relationship would be even stronger. And that's exactly what has happened!

A few weeks later, we were driving back from a training project. She told me that while she had been cleaning her inbox, she came across many of the emails we exchanged during the collaboration that was at the center of our earlier dispute.

"You were right," she said. "In my anger, I forgot to take our history into consideration. I'm truly sorry!"

"My salutation is to him who sees me imperfect and loves me." These words were penned by Nobel Prize winner Rabindranath Tagore to his dear friend, Albert Einstein.[4] They powerfully encapsulate what it means to act like a Bridge Builder.

Everyone wants to be seen and heard. Acting like Bridge Builders means that we see and hear people because we value our relationships with them.

I'd love to tell you that I *always* act like Bridge Builder and that all conflict always ends with a happy story. I would be lying.

The truth is that we've all seen damaged relationships—and we are often as much to blame as the other person. But building bridges isn't about perfection—it's about intention. And when we act like Bridge Builders, even after we've blown it, most damaged relationships can be repaired over time.

Bottom line: Acting like Bridge Builders means we're willing to take action *before we feel like it*—with empathy, authenticity, and respect. This was the case in the confrontation I experienced with my friend and colleague. We both acted to preserve the relationship, even though neither of us felt like it—at least not at first.

Acting like a Bridge Builder rarely is our first instinct, but stepping into that uncomfortable space is worth the pain.

Bridge Builder Notes

Nobody really wants to act like a Bridge Builder.

- Do you agree or disagree with the previous statement? Why?
- Can you remember a time when acting like a Bridge Builder helped you preserve a valuable relationship?

Blueprint: Acting Like a Bridge Builder

- Listen like a Bridge Builder (refer to previous section).
- Be fully present (put away the phone).
- Express yourself authentically, but with respect.
- Put the relationship above tasks, feelings, and agendas.
- Give others permission to tell you the truth—to be vulnerable—and don't penalize them for it.
- Assume positive intentions, even when emotions are running high.
- Confront with the intention to restore and strengthen relationships.
- Be patient when others don't see things your way.
- Remember that it takes time to strengthen relationships. Don't shortcut the process.
- Protect others and the culture from toxic people who refuse to act like Bridge Builders.
- Lean in. Choose to trust and be vulnerable.

It's worth repeating that acting like a Bridge Builder is not a matter of perfection, but a matter of intention. And intention means making a choice and acting on that choice. The more we step into actions that foster connection, the more those choices become part of who we are.

Principle 4: Talk Like a Bridge Builder

Bridge Builders are persuasive communicators—whether they communicate with one person or in front of a large audience. Persuasion happens when we reach our audience's hearts and minds, ultimately influencing movement in behavior and ways of thinking.

In the next section, I will discuss the SUPERB tools Bridge Builders use to communicate persuasively. But for now, let's consider a time-proven idea.

According to Aristotle, persuasion happens when we incorporate three types of arguments into our communication: ethical (ethos), emotional (pathos), and logical (logos). These three types of appeals play influential roles in business and personal communication.

The ethical appeal

"Character may almost be called the most effective means of persuasion," said Aristotle. Ethos, then, is based upon the communicator's personal credibility, character, and shared values with the audience. If the audience feels they can't trust you because you lack credibility and integrity, building a bridge to them will be impossible—regardless of the passion you bring to your message. Mistrust means your message will be dismissed.

Likewise, credentials alone, without character, will not help your credibility. In the parable, Daniel realizes that building credibility with his audience requires more than his father's name and his own prestigious credentials. Depending on the situation, your credentials, education, and track record will be essential to building your credibility. But character, shared values, and transparency also influence your ability to gain credibility and garner the trust of your audience.

Every audience, consciously or subconsciously, wants to know whether you and your ideas can be trusted. Knowing your audience— what they care about and how they think—and being intentional about communicating ethos can make all the difference in whether or not you reach their hearts, minds, or both.

The emotional appeal

Pathos comes into play when you stir the audience's heart—their emotions, but also their appetite for creativity. Marketers know that audiences are more likely to buy their products when they form an emotional attachment to that product. As a general rule, data and facts alone appeal to the mind—not the heart, unless you've made sure the data tells a story the audience cares about.

In the parable, Tammy and Chad communicate data that tells a clear story Daniel cares about: how to lead a thriving organization. As the story unfolds, Daniel begins to pay attention, because the story behind the data helps him picture a brighter future. We also see how Michael makes an even stronger connection with Daniel during his keynote by sharing a story that triggers his emotions and desires.

Bridge Builders are masterful storytellers. Daniel eventually discovers that Story and vulnerability are vital to connect with the audience's imagination, creativity, and emotions—the way data alone can't.

The logical appeal

Logos helps audiences make sense of information and data. Structure is the most powerful tool we have to improve logical appeal—the reason why stories are also effective communication tools to package information.

Simply put, audiences are wired to listen for a clear opening, middle, and end. But far too many communicators overwhelm their audiences with disorganized messages, as if to say, "Here's all the data. Now you figure it out." When you take the time to figure out the story behind the data, you've taken the first step to building a bridge to your audience's need for clarity and logical structure.

Daniel discovers the importance of organizing his ideas with his audience in mind. Being a champion for the audience finally helps him realize he must package his message in a way that is most helpful and useful for the audience.

In the illustration that follows, you can see how the three appeals connect with the audience in tangible ways. When our communication flows from an ethical appeal, we are rewarded with our audience's trust. When our communication flows from an emotional appeal, we evoke an emotional response from our audience. And when our communication delivers information with a logical appeal, audiences clearly understand where we want to take them.

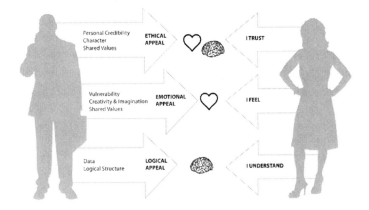

The Blueprint that follows will help you begin to improve your credibility (ethos) so you can connect with your audience at a higher level. When you get to the SUPERB tools, you'll learn practical ways to be more persuasive and reach the hearts and minds of your audience by incorporating the other two persuasive appeals.

 Bridge Builder Notes

"If you wish to win a man over to your ideas, first make him your friend." —**Abraham Lincoln**

- When was the last time someone persuaded you?
- When was the last time you persuaded someone else?
- What role did each of the three appeals play in each instance?

Blueprint: Improving Your Credibility

Bottom line—becoming a more credible communicator is part of the process of building bridges. The more credible you are, the easier it'll be to reach the **hearts** and **minds** of your audience.

- Clarify your credibility: Audiences will probably search for your name online. What will they find when they find your website, your social media profile, and the messages you post online? Consider how the wrong information, outdated information, or no information can hurt your credibility among the audiences you are trying to reach.
- Let others brag about you: A powerful introduction that outlines your accomplishments can win an audience before you even step in front of them. Craft a script others can use and throw modesty to the wind.

- Think "Story Structure": Audiences understand messages when they have a clear beginning, middle, and end; so inject this simple structure when sharing ideas.

- Incorporate concrete and vivid language: Learn to paint vivid images by using concrete language. For example: Steve Jobs knew that—"An MP3 player with one gigabyte of memory" was an abstract concept that would not help his audience build an emotional connection to the iPod. "One thousand songs in your pocket," however, did.

- Grow comfortable with vulnerability: Audiences trust and connect with authentic communicators. Appropriate self-disclosure and the willingness to admit you don't know everything can build a powerful bridge to the audience.

Principle 5: Lead Like a Bridge Builder

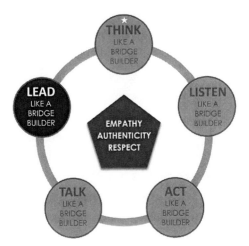

Bridge Builder leaders stand out because they have a compelling message to share, have a keen understanding of human nature, excel at building bridges to the hearts and minds of their target audiences with empathy and authenticity, and do what other leaders aren't willing to do.

Bridge Builder leaders know who they are and where they're going. They have vision and conviction—despite their limitations. Power players, critics, and skeptics don't intimidate them, so they're willing to push the envelope and challenge the status quo. Bill Porter, the inspiration behind the film *Door to Door*, is a good example. He became the top salesman for Watkins Incorporated—despite his cerebral palsy—building bridges, one customer at a time, overcoming his initial apprehension.

Bridge Builder leaders invest in vision and culture. They understand that their ability to build bridges to the hearts and minds of their audiences is only the beginning. As leaders, they understand that a team of people who share common attitudes, values, and vision is unstoppable; so they invest in building cultures where Bridge Builders can thrive. They don't sacrifice culture over talent—even if they can make an immediate impact on the bottom line—ensuring that the corporate vision doesn't leak. Tony Hsieh, Zappos.com founder and CEO, has built one of the most successful and lucrative companies on this principle. "Superstars who can make a significant contribution to the company's bottom line but don't fit with the corporate culture get canned."[5]

Bridge Builder leaders aren't ashamed to lead with heart. Some call it servant leadership. Empathic leadership. Or the willingness to be seen as you truly are. Leading with heart spells "vulnerability"—what author and scholar Brené Brown calls the "birthplace of innovation, creativity, and change."

Take Sheryl Samberg, Facebook's Chief Operations Officer. She's one of the most influential executives in the world today. Certainly sharing her personal struggles and insecurities about leading as a woman could do little to add to her credibility. But by writing *Lean In*—Sandberg's response to her own question, "What would you do if you weren't afraid?"—her influence has skyrocketed to new and unexpected heights. Why? Because she became human to millions of women and leaders around the world. Because she came out and said what millions of people were already thinking. Ken Blanchard puts it best: "Leaders need to be bearers of hope, show their vulnerability, and operate by a set of values."[6]

Bridge Builders leaders seek feedback, because they understand that everyone has blind spots and that others have valuable data that can positively impact their effectiveness as leaders and decision makers. Bridge Builder leaders also understand how difficult it is to gather valuable feedback, because many people shy away from sharing or share in a way that isn't productive. For that reason, they intentionally develop systems and cultures that facilitate the gathering and sharing of feedback. Like Ken Blanchard, they believe that "feedback is the breakfast of champions."

Consider Andy Stanley, one of the most influential and effective global leaders in the world of church ministry. Each Sunday, more than thirty-three thousand people attend five Atlanta-area churches he leads, and his messages on leadership and sermon content get downloaded over two million times every month. A great deal of his effectiveness as a Bridge Builder leader stems from the fact that he has built and nurtured a culture of feedback. He challenges his leaders to seek feedback by starting with a simple question: "If you were me, what would you do differently?"[7]

Bridge Builder leaders don't build bridges to everyone—nor do they want to—because doing so would require diluting or compromising their core message. Martin Luther King, Jr. and Margaret Thatcher are good examples. They deeply felt the weight that overpowered the people they were trying to reach (empathy) and presented their messages with conviction, no holds barred (authenticity). They didn't reach every person, but they built bridges to the hearts and minds of enough people to achieve their vision.

It's important to point out that Bridge Builder leaders don't intentionally alienate their audience. That's what ordinary communicators do through personal diatribes, manufacturing controversy for the sake of ratings, or by posting their unedited thoughts on social media. Bridge Builders inevitably separate themselves from certain audiences, because the integrity of their message alone—shared with empathy and authenticity—organically elicits responses from critics, cynics, or those who respectfully disagree or decline to follow.

Bridge Builder Notes

Bridge Builder Leadership isn't about perfection—it's about intention.

- How intentional are you about exercising the attributes listed above?
- What attributes do you think need more attention?
- What Bridge Builder leaders do you admire that emulate the attributes listed above?

How to Begin Leading Like a Bridge Builder

It bears repeating that leading like a Bridge Builder is not a matter of position or perfection. Anyone who has influence over others—extrinsic or intrinsic—can lead like a Bridge Builder.

Many excellent books address the subject of how to be a more effective leader, and selected titles are listed on the Bridge Builder Book Resource Website. The Bridge Builder Approach is an additional and valuable resource that provides you with two powerful tools: the Bridge Builder Manifesto and the online SUPERB Assessment.

The Bridge Builder Manifesto is a tool for leaders who are looking to improve their influence and ability to lead more effectively and authentically—at home or at work. You'll get an abbreviated version in the section that follows, but you can learn more about it in the Book Resources Website.

The online SUPERB Communication Assessment facilitates self-awareness through feedback. The assessment is most valuable when you allow others to respond to it on your behalf, because their feedback will give you objective data about how you come across to others.

Resources Beyond the Book in the Book Resources Website is a further invitation to continue this conversation.

Book Resources Website
LeadersBuildBridges.com

CHAPTER 41

THE SUPERB TOOLS

B ridge Builders master six tools in order to reach their audience's
hearts and minds. They're easy to remember because they
spell the word SUPERB. These simple tools make it possible
for your communication to have the ethical, emotional, and logical
appeals we discussed earlier.

- **Story** is the single most important tool in your Bridge Builder
  toolbox. In fact, the other five tools exist to support it. Story
  connects with the mind because it delivers information
  in a clear and logical structure. It connects with the heart
  by evoking the audience's emotions and imagination
  through plot, tension, character development, and
  concrete imagery.
- **Usefulness** is the WIIFM factor—"What's in it for me?"
  Audiences want and need to understand why they should care
  about your message and how they fit into your story.

173

- **Passion** enlivens meaning. It infuses data and stories with spiritual-like energy that can't be communicated through data or structure. Passion connects with audiences at a deeper level. It taps into their desire to be part of something greater than themselves—something that can help them change the world.
- **Empathy** is the ability to stand in your audience's shoes, see through their eyes, think through their perspective, and feel with their hearts. Incidentally, empathy is the tool that facilitates authenticity and respect—elements at the heart of all Bridge Builder Communication.
- **Reliability** is your credibility (ethos) as a communicator and as a leader—whether it comes from your credentials, reputation, or the soundness of your work and data.
- **Brevity** is your ability to convey meaning with as few words as possible—no more and no less than needed to convey your message with integrity and authenticity.

The following graphic shows how each of the SUPERB tools connects with your audience's heart and mind.

In my experience, most individuals have a tendency to use (or overuse) some of the tools, while neglecting others. **Feedback**—what

Ken Blanchard calls "the breakfast of champions"—is essential to take your influence to the next level. Feedback transforms you from an "ordinary" communicator into a "superb" communicator. The online SUPERB Assessment is a tool specifically designed to help you gather concrete feedback from your audience, a mentor, or a coach. You can access a copy at LeadersBuildBridges.com.

 Bridge Builder Notes

"We work in a first-draft culture. Type an e-mail. Send. Write a blog entry. Post. Whip up some slides. Speak. But it's in crafting and recrafting—in iteration and rehearsal—that excellence emerges."
—**Nancy Duarte**, *HBR Guide to Persuasive Presentations*

- How much time do you spend preparing your communication, so that you can reach the hearts and minds of your audiences?
- At first glance, which of the six SUPERB tools do you tend to use with ease? Which is harder for you to use?
- What new opportunities would open up for you if you decided to invest more time in preparation?

Story

Thanks to breakthroughs in neuroscience, we now know that our brains are wired for story. Cognitive scientist Robert C. Schank puts it this way, "Humans are not ideally set up to understand logic; they are ideally set up to understand stories."[8] In short, we make sense of the world through story and story structure.

But what exactly is story?

Simply put—story is the journey of a **character who overcomes obstacles in order to get what she wants**. A character can be a man, a woman, a team, a product, an idea, a cause, or an organization.

Story and Business Communication

Business professionals who use storytelling techniques to connect with their audiences achieve their goals. Branding experts and marketers craft compelling stories that make us buy their products.

Some of the most successful organizations in the world intentionally leverage storytelling. Southwest Airlines. Microsoft. Disney. Costco. FedEx. Procter & Gamble. Bristol-Myers-Squibb. NASA. From the biotech world to finance, savvy business leaders know that story is also a powerful leadership tool.

In *Lead with Story*, Paul Smith shares many compelling examples: At Nike all senior executives see themselves as "corporate storytellers"; 3M banned all bullet points years ago with "strategic narratives"; Procter & Gamble has invested heavily in training their executives with storytelling techniques.[9]

But not everyone gets the picture—not at first. Ron, a seasoned engineer but apprehensive presenter I coached a few years ago, was one of them. "Sharing a story is just not going to fly with my audience," he told me. "The executive team I'm presenting to expects me to share the hard data—without gimmicks."

Fortunately, Ron, like Daniel in the parable, came around when he realized that story is not a gimmick, but the perfect structure for organizing technical information, and also a way to humanize it. Geoffrey Berwind, corporate storytelling consultant, puts it best: "For too long, companies have relied on offering change ideas only by supplying data, numbers, statistics, analytics, and so on . . . There's a well-known marketing axiom that 'people buy from people they know, like and trust.' . . . I've seen that there is simply no more impactful way to have that occur than through the strategic use of storytelling."[10]

Story structure in business communication, at the most basic level, involves a compelling and focused **opening**, an organized **middle**, and a purposeful **close**—all of which exist to support **ONE** distinctive message or idea.

Strategic Storytelling

Strategic storytelling simply means that you use storytelling techniques to serve the needs of your audience and to facilitate productive dialogue. The stories you tell must fit the occasion, the content, and the audience.

A story need not be elaborate for it to be effective. A useful and brief single-sentence story, for example, can be the most effective way to confront someone whose behavior is disrupting the organization— "When you show up late to meetings the team loses steam and creativity, because we have to stop the flow of ideas to bring you up to speed."

Bridge Builders are constantly adding stories to their communication toolbox. What type of stories? Annette Simmons, one of my favorite Bridge Builders and author of *The Story Factor*, teaches that everyone should be able to tell six distinct stories:

- **Who I Am Stories**: These are the stories that illustrate the qualities that earn you the right to influence others. They tell of time, place, or events that provide evidence that you possess those qualities. Daniel's wheel story is a powerful example of how *Who I Am* stories build credibility and connect with the audience.

- **Why I Am Here Stories**: These are the stories that answer the audience's internal objections about your motives. Before they ask, "What's in it for me?" they want to know "What's in it for YOU." For example, Daniel is always wondering why Michael has allowed him to "look under the MonikerTech hood." He finally gets his answer when Michael shares a story about golfing with Daniel's father.

- **Vision Stories**: "Where there's no vision, people perish," says the popular proverb. It's true. Vision stories keep the vision tank full, because it is constantly leaking. For example, Lynda's simple "Get on the ball" story helped refuel Daniel's vision tank when it was running empty.

- **Values in Action Stories**: How do you communicate values like integrity, work ethic, perseverance, and empathy? When it comes to abstract or subjective ideals, showing is more powerful than telling. Annette Simmons reminds us that showing by example is the best way. Story is a close second. Stories like the Good Samaritan or Michael's keynote story are examples of *Values in Action* stories.

- **I Know What You Are Thinking Stories**: When audiences make up their minds or close their minds to our ideas, chances are they are holding on to valid or invalid objections. Stories that illustrate you *understand* their objections and address them head-on invites them to relax and give you the benefit of the doubt. All through the story we see Chris anticipating Daniel's apprehension and addressing it with timely illustrations like the Coronado Bay Bridge. Daniel internalizes this lesson and ultimately shares his wheel story to address the board's apprehension about his work ethic and ability to lead the company successfully by building bridges.

- **Teaching Stories**: Why do people immediately connect with stories like the Good Samaritan? Simmons says it best—"a 'teaching story' transports the listener into an experience that lets him or her see, smell, taste, touch, hear, and feel a real situation in all its ambiguity, time pressures and real life issues. It imprints into the listeners mind a 'never do this' or 'this is how it is done' memory that can equal a true experience."[11] In the parable, Tammy and Chad use their "CT, the communication terrorist" story to find common ground with Daniel and drive key points home.

To Simmons' list, I'd like to add one more category I will describe in more detail in the next section:

- **Bridge Builder Manifesto Stories**: These are defining stories that serve as a plumb line, aligning you to your most authentic leadership as a Bridge Builder. Incidentally, they can serve a purpose within one or more of the six categories above—as is the case with Daniel's wheel story. But whether you choose to share them with others or not, these stories are stories you tell yourself—over and over again. They remind you what it looks like to be true to yourself and why being completely true to who you are is the only way to garner the trust and loyalty of those you want to reach.

Strategic storytelling is often a matter of employing story structure techniques to build connections, to improve results, or to foster more creativity and innovation. For example, planning a meeting around a story timeline can turn a stale meeting into a breeding ground for ideas and solutions to problems.

Imagine designing the meeting around the basic definition of story: a hero (Product X) that wants something (reach consumer market Y) and must overcome obstacles (competition and limited marketing budget) in order to reach the goal. What do you think will yield a better outcome: a traditional, linear meeting agenda? Or, a storyline approach that allows for strategic conflict and resolution? Take my word—chuck the agenda. If the idea intrigues you, download a Meeting Storyline Blueprint from the Book Resources Website.

Bottom line, story, story structure, and strategic storytelling are tools. You are the Bridge Builder, and it's up to you to master the tools and use them intentionally to achieve maximum results.

Bridge Builder Notes

"Long before the first formal business was established . . . the six most powerful words in any language were, 'Let me tell you a story.'"
—**Matthews & Wacker**, quoted by Paul Smith in *Lead with Story.*

- What role do story, story structure, or strategic storytelling play in your communication? In your organization?
- What are some of the most influential stories you have heard?
- What are some of the most influential stories you have shared?

Blueprint: Using Story Strategically

Bridge Builders constantly build their story repertoires. It's an intentional process I call String-Saving. It's never too late to begin collecting and honing stories.

- Read and collect stories. *The Story Factor, Lead with Story,* and *True North* are three books I highly recommend for inspiration and application. I've listed their bibliographical information in the Notes section.
- Learn from others. The birth and popularity of TED presentations have given us unlimited access to great storytellers. Listen to them. Listen to their stories. Learn from them.
- Collect personal stories. Evaluate them and consider where they fit within the seven story types I listed earlier. The Bridge Builder Manifesto section provides suggestions to mine for personal defining stories.
- Write the stories before you share them. The writing process will help you organize the facts and eliminate superfluous details. It also will help you gain a clearer perspective about

their significance. Ask yourself: How should the story begin? How should the middle be organized? How should it end?

- Practice and get feedback. Great storytelling starts with preparation, practice, and feedback from others.
- Keep adding stories to your repertoire. Organize them and tag them so they're easy to access. Evernote is valuable digital tool I use for this purpose.

Usefulness

I'm a big fan of *Shark Tank*, the popular television show where entrepreneurs get a few minutes to pitch their product to a group of investors (the sharks). I have yet to see an entrepreneur who wasn't passionate about his product. However, passion alone isn't going to make someone hand you thousands of dollars.

The sharks, for example, want to know whether the product is marketable and potentially profitable—because it solves a significant problem—and whether they'll be able to work with the presenter. And when the presenters don't make this information clear, they're bombarded with questions—at best—or contempt at worst.

Most communicators don't have the luxury of access to dialogue and questions to clarify a confusing message. Consider these costly examples:

- The potential client who leaves your website because information is hard to find.
- The potential partner who stops reading an important email because it goes on and on and on.
- The executive team that tunes you out during a key presentation because busy slides and data overload bury the most important part of the message.
- The audience that tunes you out because your message is disorganized and confusing.

Usefulness is about solving problems. It's about answering the audience's questions, quickly and succinctly: What's in it for me? How can this information benefit me? Usefulness doesn't always need to be pragmatic. Inspiration can be useful when the problem is discouragement. Providing useful communication comes down to knowing as much as we can about our audience, because the idea of a "captive audience" is an illusion.

Audiences will not be held hostage to what they perceive to be useless information. Just because they're physically in front of you or your message doesn't mean they're mentally engaged. It's up to you to grab their attention quickly by showing how your message solves a problem for them or facilitates practical transformation.

Remember, your message is competing with thousands—even millions—of other messages. Make yours useful and relevant to your audience, and it will stand out.

Bridge Builder Notes

Everyone has a problem that needs solving.

- How would your communication change today if your sole purpose were to solve someone's problem?
- Consider the audience you are trying to reach with your message. What problem are they hoping to solve and how can you make that possible?

Blueprint: Delivering More Useful Messages

Because usefulness is about solving a tangible problem for the audience, it's important to know your audience as much as you can. When you begin with questions about your audience, you will be more prepared to deliver a message that is useful.

- Who's my audience?
- What do they care about?
- What don't they care about?
- How does my message, product, or idea solve their problem?
- How can I present my message as a solution to their problem?
- How can I make the message more memorable?
- What questions are they likely to ask me?
- What questions are likely to come to mind?
- If they forget everything I say—what is the number one thing I want them to remember?

Passion

Sylvia and Kent have a problem.

I met Sylvia, a junior manager at a large financial institution, when her manager decided that communication coaching would help her improve her executive presence. He knew she was talented and dedicated and had tremendous potential to grow with the company. But the feedback she was getting from executives after presenting or facilitating meetings wasn't helping her credibility and upward mobility in the organization.

Unapproachable. Stoic. Indifferent. Lacks energy. Not confident. The feedback boiled down to a lack of passion—or so I thought.

Kent's story is the complete opposite. He's a young and energetic professional who's being groomed for a leadership position that will require substantial public speaking, both to teach and inspire his team. His boss asked me to observe his latest presentation and provide feedback that could help him become a more effective leader.

Unapologetically extroverted, Kent exudes passion from every pore. When he's presenting, he's fun to watch. "It's like watching a Facebook feed," an audience member commented on his presentation style, probably because the various stories and points in Kent's message flashed through our eyes and ears so rapidly without a perceivable core message to tie everything together. In Kent's case, passion takes precedence over clarity and meeting the audience's needs.

Passion can be a needed life-sustaining rain or a destructive downpour.

When passion is paired with a compelling story that speaks directly to the hearts and minds of the audience, it makes our messages hard to resist. It enhances the story, evokes our creative and emotional senses, makes us want to listen, and inspires us to take action. And here lies the problem for Sylvia and for Kent.

Sylvia needed to convey passion, because she actually was passionate about her work and the contributions her team was making to the company's bottom line. Her challenge was that her subdued, quiet personality faded into the background in a workplace of type A personalities. Sylvia didn't have a passion problem; she had a perception problem. Coaching her meant helping her understand her audience and meet their needs.

Fortunately, Sylvia was able to make simple but significant tweaks in her communication style that helped her meet the expectations of her audience and come across as more confident and passionate, without compromising her uniqueness.

It's important to point out that American audiences, in particular, associate passion with energy. As a rule, energy conveys passion and confidence. But don't let that discourage you if your personality tends to be subdued, like Sylvia's. You, too, can project energy and passion by adopting the strategies in the Blueprint that follows.

Kent, on the other hand, had a different problem. He's dynamite to be sure, but he also has a hard time meeting the needs of his audience—who are desperately trying to keep up with him. In his case, passion becomes a tsunami that overwhelms the audience. He tries to create an experience—not only for the audience but also for himself—and wastes the first few minutes of his presentation trying to get an audible response from an audience that may or may not be ready to meet his level of exuberance.

Kent has the potential to become an extraordinary communicator by redirecting some of his passion to his preparation. Once he does that, he'll be more sensitive to the needs of his audience, craft a story that is easier to digest, and temper his exuberance so that it energizes the audience enough to act on the important message he wants to communicate—without overwhelming them.

Bottom line—passion is infectious and easily reaches the hearts of audiences. But passion alone is not enough to move an audience to action.

Blueprint: Conveying Passion (for Low-Key Bridge Builders)

- Mirror your audience's energy level without sacrificing your authentic communication style.
- Project your voice—imagine you are talking to someone at the end of the room.
- When presenting, move intentionally, rather than standing in one place. In some corporate cultures, standing up when presenting is not the norm. Be willing to rock the boat when appropriate. Or take up more space by sitting straight (don't slouch). Lean in and open up your body by owning the chair or the space.
- Make eye contact. Smile.
- Invite feedback from a trusted source. Ask for specific observations about how you convey passion and confidence.
- Practice a two-minute power pose. Go to LeadersBuildBridges. com/passion to see how the research of social scientist Amy Cuddy can make you come across as more confident by adopting a two-minute power pose before facing your audience.

Blueprint: Moderating Passion
(for High-Energy Bridge Builders)

- Make it about your audience, not yourself. Mirror your audience's energy level as you begin to communicate, slowly raising your level to match your authentic style (as appropriate).

- Remember that introverts express passion differently than you do, so get to know them before you alienate them. Consider reading Susan Cain's *Quiet: The Power of Introverts in a World That Can't Stop Talking*. From her introduction: "At least one-third of the people we know are introverts. They are the ones who prefer listening to speaking, reading to partying; who innovate and create but dislike self-promotion; who favor working on their own over brainstorming in teams. Although they are often labeled 'quiet,' it is to introverts that we owe many of the great contributions to society—from van Gogh's *Sunflowers* to the invention of the personal computer."

- Adjust your pacing to match your purpose: Is your purpose to entertain or to educate? Is it to motivate or to teach? If the audience needs to learn and internalize key concepts, then slowing down at key junctures of your communication will help make key points memorable.

- Don't slack on preparation. If you are presenting, open and close with purpose. Structure your message so that it's easy to follow. Many extroverted communicators, who initially shun structure, discover that structure actually frees them up to be themselves.

- Get feedback from those who can help you become a passionate—but effective—communicator.

- When addressing mixed audiences—extroverts and introverts—aim to meet them both in a middle ground.

Bridge Builder Notes

Passion is infectious and easily reaches the hearts of audiences. But passion alone is not enough to move an audience to action.

- Sylvia and Kent represent opposite sides of the passion spectrum. Who most closely resembles you?
- What bullet points in the two previous blueprints are most beneficial to help you convey or moderate passion when you communicate?

Empathy

Empathy is the ability to stand in your audience's shoes, see through their eyes, think through their perspective, and feel with their hearts. Empathy allows you to become a **champion** for that audience through all you say and do—especially if you expect to build bridges to their hearts and minds.

Empathy has always been a vital element of effective communication, but the arrival of today's social consumer demands for more intentional empathy.

If you lead an organization that needs to build bridges to today's social and mobile audiences—if they are your customers and stakeholders—listen to what David F. Giannetto has to say: "Today's consumers are smarter than they have ever been, utilizing social media and mobile technology as part of their decision-making process, and doing so in a way that gives them the most options at the lowest price. But these are only the superficial changes. The underlying evolution in consumer behavior is having a more significant impact upon how organizations structure and utilize the people, processes, information, and technologies that touch the consumer."[12]

Make no mistake—even if the word "empathy" is left out of the conversation—empathy is at the heart of learning how to engage each and every audience you want to reach.

Studies show that empathy and empathy-driven policies in the workplace positively affect performance, employee engagement, and customer satisfaction—and not just in the United States. When empathy trickles through business communication, the results are undeniable.[13] Consider the following scenarios:

Southwest Airlines: "Without a heart, it's just a machine" is not just a new corporate slogan; it's one of the clearest examples of empathetic communication at the corporate level. It's a constant internal and external reminder that a people-centric culture drives a people-centric business practices.[14]

Zappos.com: in *Delivering Happiness,* Zappos founder and CEO, Tony Hsieh, exemplifies why "Powered by Service" is not just a corporate tagline. It's a declaration of empathy, which has permeated the culture and brand that puts family (employees and customers) first. Some companies are fast to broadcast customer testimonials and hide complaints. Not Zappos. In fact, they publish both under the following message: "Compliments (as well as complaints) from our customers are considered treasures here at Zappos. We're always listening with open and attentive ears . . ."[15]

Google: In *How Google Works,* Eric Schmidt and Jonathan Rosenberg candidly reveal the lessons and secrets behind Google's success. Empathy may not be how they would choose to describe Google's approach to managing and retaining human capital, but actions speak louder than words.

One example stands out when the authors identify the challenges associated with managing "smart creatives," a new breed of employees who, Schmidt and Rosenberg believe "are the key to achieving success in the Internet Century." Smart creatives possess deep technical knowledge in their field, overflowing creative intelligence and ability, as well as business savvy. They are creative communicators and independent thinkers who work hard and are willing to challenge the status quo.

How does empathy come into play with managing these employees? "If you can't tell someone how to think, then you have to learn to manage the environment where they think. And make it a place where they want to come every day." One way Google does this is by establishing a culture of Yes. "No is like a tiny death to smart creatives . . . Enough nos, and smart creatives stop asking and start heading to the exits."[16]

Google is the perfect example of how empathy in a corporate culture can work. And how it can be implemented without "touchy-feely" activities.

These are just a handful of examples of how empathy plays a role in Bridge Builder Communication. You can find more examples in the Book Resources Website. But before we move on to the next subject, let me point out that empathy is intricately connected with vulnerability—and that is both good and terrifying. Southwest Airlines is both praised and ridiculed by their efforts to lead with heart. Zappos's openness to share both the praise and the criticism of customers can't be easy. And establishing a culture of "yes" for the sake of smart creatives can be a messy proposition.

So are empathy and vulnerability worth the investment?

Dr. Brené Brown, who studies human connection—our ability to empathize and to be vulnerable—gives us a clue. Shortly after rising to international notoriety, following her 2010 TEDx Talk, "The Power of Vulnerability," Fortune 500 companies flooded her with invitations to speak on innovation, creativity, and change—as long as she didn't mention vulnerability. Yes, we can agree that empathy and vulnerability are two words not fully welcome in business settings. Her response: "Vulnerability is the birthplace of innovation, creativity, and change. To create is to make something that has never existed before. There's nothing more vulnerable than that. Adaptability to change is all about vulnerability."[17]

Bottom line: Empathy (paired with vulnerability) has never been more important than today to capture the attention of our target audiences—customers and stakeholders included.

Bridge Builder Notes

You can't walk in someone else's shoes if you are still wearing your own.

- How does empathy and vulnerability relate to the previous statement?
- What role does empathy play in the communication you deliver on a day-to-day basis?
- If you were asked to design policies guided by empathy, what changes would you make in your organization?

Blueprint: Writing a Letter of Complaint (with Empathy)

If more businesses emulated the Bridge Builder customer service practices of companies like Nordstrom, Southwest, and Zappos—to name a few—complaints would be a thing of the past.

A while back I was extremely dissatisfied with the customer service I received after purchasing an online software service. I knew that a refund was fair, but I was getting nowhere with customer service.

I could have let the money go, since the aggravation of working with customer service had surpassed the value of the refund. But as I thought about it, I realized I needed to follow my own advice and consider this an opportunity to approach my complaint with empathy.

I told myself that if one of my customers had been treated the way I had been treated, I would want to know and have the opportunity to make it right.

After a quick search, I found the company's CEO on LinkedIn. I sent him a request to connect, and to my delight he accepted within the hour. Now it was time to present my case—so I began by asking the question, "If I were in his shoes, what kind of letter would I pay attention to?"

I'll warn you that writing a short five-hundred-word letter—that tells a story with empathy—is neither an easy nor a fast endeavor. Was it worth it? Read on and be the judge.

Dear Randy,

Thank you for accepting my connection request.

Today I'm connecting as a long-time advocate and consumer of the ABC brand, which covers the XYZ product I recently purchased.

I decided to write because in all my years of working with global companies, I have never felt so disillusioned by a sales and customer service team as I was this week by the XYZ team.

The quick story is that I reached out to your customer service unit requesting cancellation and refund for the remainder of my XYZ subscription (Jan-Nov) because it isn't the right solution for our business at this time. Without even a thread of consideration or fair dialogue, your customer service representative shut me down. My hope is that you will see that although my request for a $300+ refund is reasonable, this note addresses a bigger issue within your organization:

On November 14th, I visited the XYZ website and signed up for a free trial. Within 60 seconds, Tom Speedy, one of your sales reps, called my cell phone. His quick response and "special offer" were so impressive that I paid in advance for a one-year $400 subscription within 10 minutes. We laughed about his comment that customers are more likely to buy if you get to them as soon as they show interest.

A little over 30 days into my subscription, it became clear that XYZ is not the right fit for my business at this time. Clearly, I made an emotional decision with the help of a savvy salesman. However, I'm now appalled that a company bearing the ABC brand can cling to a "no refund policy" so vehemently without listening to reason and evidence.

While it took Tom only minutes to nail the sale, it has taken me many wasted hours and emails to present my case.

And although the terms of the quote are on my side, Tom's dismissive response continues to be: "We give no refunds to our customers, but I'll be happy to give you free training." It's clear that I haven't been heard, as training has never been the issue.

Randy, this is not a note from someone who makes a habit of cancelling services or complaining. I have referred clients to XYZ. I'm in business to make a profit myself. And I understand that policies are published for a reason but are flexible enough when principle and people are more important.

I know that you or someone else in your organization can make this right . . . if you want to. I'm hopeful that this is an isolated incident that does not define the character and business practices of XYZ. I know that one retroactive refund will not break your company. It will, however, gain an advocate and one more potential client down the road when the time is right.

I don't know if you check your LinkedIn box regularly, so I will follow up with an email in a few days if I don't hear back.

With kind regards I thank you in advance for your consideration,
Maria Keckler

In less than ten hours, XYZ's customer service rep wrote me back, informing me that a refund had been processed. Randy, the CEO, responded briefly, thanking me for the note and saying that he welcomed my input.

The story of empathy is spelled out in the Golden Rule—treat others the way you want to be treated. We all have experienced or witnessed—at least once—when an angry customer unleashes his wrath on an unsuspecting employee. Likewise, we have seen wounded customers, who have been sliced and diced by rude and careless "customer service" associates.

Although you may not be writing a letter of complaint in the near future, the lessons apply to other business communication.

Audiences respond when they know you care about their perspective, when they feel you've taken their unique set of circumstances into consideration and that you're willing to communicate your thoughts and ideas with respect.

If you have been putting off writing a letter to make your case, follow these tips I used to craft mine:

- Consider your audience's perspective before you begin drafting. Truly put yourself in their shoes and ask yourself, "How would I appreciate being approached?"
- Organize your ideas by writing out the story you want to share (know that you'll revise it, probably more than once). Start by putting your ideas down on paper first.
- Clarify—first for yourself—what is the bottom line message you want to communicate. Spell it out up front and then fill in the details.
- Revise by asking yourself whether the letter qualifies as a SUPERB message: by communicating a clear **story**; by providing **useful** information for your reader; by communicating **passion** combined with **empathy**; by making sure your depiction of people and events involved is **reliable**; by deleting the fluff and keeping it as **brief** as possible.
- Breathe and put the letter away for 24 hours before you hit *Send*. Don't be surprised that you decide to make a few tweaks after you read it with new eyes.
- Know when to continue the conversation (if you don't get the desired response) and when it's time to surrender. Not every response is favorable, and you'll have to decide what would a Bridge Builder say or do next?

Blueprint: Facilitating Empathy
- Listen empathetically (See Principle #2).
- Consider your message from your audience's perspective.

- Make eye contact and aim to really see your audience.
- Put away your technology. Be fully present.
- Mirror your audience—if you sense confusion, pause and slow down. If they smile, smile back.
- Let emotions subside before you discuss hot topics.
- Take the time to think about what you want to say and how you would like others to address you if you were in their shoes.
- Be willing to be vulnerable.
- Be willing to surrender when the other person is not ready to build a bridge.

Reliability

Emmanuel was in charge of introducing a relatively well-known speaker at a large event. The speaker was speaking to three different audiences over two days and had emailed his bio ahead of time, which he wanted Emmanuel to use during his introduction.

"I made the mistake of winging my introduction and saying, 'Ladies and gentlemen, welcome Paul to the stage, a man who needs no introduction.'"

"Big mistake," Emmanuel later shared with his team during a team meeting. Not only did Paul chastise him—nicely—between sessions, but he also taught him a lesson about being perceived as a reliable and credible communicator. "The introduction is not for me—to stroke my ego," he told Emmanuel. "The introduction is for the audience—it prepares them to listen without being distracted by doubts about my credentials."

Needless to say, Emmanuel nailed his second and third introductions.

Earlier we talked about the importance of ethos to connect with the audience—that's what being perceived as reliable is all about. Audiences want to know they can trust us. As we speak, they are making up their minds about our reliability and the trustworthiness of our message.

Audiences will make up their minds about the reliability of your message both by its structure (is it easy to understand?) and the credibility of your data and sources.

However, reliability can be a matter of perception. For example, if you dump all the details of your data on your audience, rather than presenting the story behind the data, they'll wonder what you might be hiding.

How you craft your communication influences how your audience perceives you and your message. Busy PowerPoint slides or grammatical errors can give the audience the impression that you don't care. Properly cite your sources, use reliable data, and be willing to address the audience's objections.

Bridge Builder Notes

We need others to point out our reliability and credibility blind spots.

- Whose message or influence have you resisted because you perceived a lack of reliability and credibility?
- How do you ensure your blind spots in this area come to the surface?

Blueprint: Improving Personal Credibility

- Ask a trusted coach or mentor to help you identify the chinks in your credibility armor.
- Don't be afraid to highlight your accomplishments when appropriate (LinkedIn profile, your personal or company website, etc.).
- Help others brag about you. Prepare a proper introduction they can use when you are going to present to their group.

- Learn to talk about yourself in sound bites. When someone asks what you do or what you are working on, don't make them regret they asked by giving them the long version. Anticipate questions, prepare succinct answers, and let them ask for more.
- Consider how vulnerability can help you improve your credibility.

Blueprint: Crafting More Credible Messages

- Figure out the story behind the data and deliver that information.
- Think "Less Is More" when it comes to visuals and complicated information.
- Have someone else review your materials before they go out.
- Whenever possible, let the audience participate in the conversation. Let them ask questions.
- Answer the question—then elaborate.
- Make eye contact with the audience.
- Cite sources.
- Be willing to say, "I don't know . . . but I can find out."

Brevity

"What doesn't add, dilutes," my friend Mary Ann Mariani likes to say. She's right!

An idea that can be expressed with one sentence should not be explained in one paragraph. A presentation that can drive the key message home in twenty minutes should not be spread out over forty minutes—even if that's the time you have been granted.

Twitter and TED presentations have forced us to communicate succinctly. Brevity is a gift—but it's costly, because it takes time to produce brief communication. Mark Twain once said, "I didn't have time to write a short letter, so I wrote a long one instead."

Enough said.

Bridge Builder Notes

"Be sincere, be brief, be seated."
                    —**Franklin D. Roosevelt**

- How do you feel about the old axiom that "less is more"?
- What is diluting your communication and ability to connect with others?

Blueprint: Delivering More with Less

- Think in tweets: Try and bottom-line your message down to a single 140-character tweet. Then make sure everything in your message supports that bottom line.
- Listen more (see Principle 2). Perhaps what you want to say so badly has been covered already.
- In written communication: Draft fearlessly. Edit mercilessly.
- In presentations: Plan analogue (avoid starting your preparation on PowerPoint, creating slides). Use a white board, a flipchart, or a paper Blueprint. Then decide what visuals will best support your story.
- Let go of pet phrases and superfluous details that don't really add to the story.
- Ask for feedback from someone who's willing to be honest.

CHAPTER 42

THE BRIDGE BUILDER MANIFESTO

A plumb line is used in building to determine whether vertical structures are perfectly vertical or perfectly true. The Bridge Builder Manifesto is your authentic leadership plumb line—your collection of personal stories, selected and refined to drive your capacity to lead like a Bridge Builder positively.

Listen to the most influential and effective leaders today, and you'll soon discover a common theme: **defining stories** that encapsulate their values, turning points, and vision for the future—stories they *choose* to believe and share. These stories define who they are, why they do what they do, and what inspires them to lead the way they do.

Bridge Builder leaders discover that believing the wrong stories ultimately will hijack their effectiveness, confidence, and ability to lead others.

Take Daniel, for example. At the beginning of his journey, he believes he'll never be an influential leader like his father was—because he believes and talks about the stories others have written about him. Those stories dictate his attitude and behavior negatively. Deep inside, he believes they're true.

Later in his journey, Daniel remembers the core stories that make him who he really is—all of which have equipped him to impact his relationships and the future of his company in positive ways.

Bottom line—the stories we believe win.

The Bridge Builder Manifesto exercise is the most powerful tool beyond this book—whether you use it for yourself or with your team— because it activates the first and most important principle: Think Like a Bridge Builder, which is why the stories we believe win.

The Manifesto Stories

Personal defining stories are the most influential stories in your Manifesto, because they speak the loudest about the core of who you are.

Not every Bridge Builder Manifesto is built upon earth-shattering stories. For example, a medical equipment sales manager once shared a moving story with her team about the time she overcame her paralyzing shyness in order to win a special trip by selling the most Girl Scout cookies in her troop. One of her sales reps later told her that hearing the story made him want to be more transparent about sharing the fears that were getting in the way of his performance.

You have defining stories. It's time to search them out intentionally.

Don't Chuck Childhood Stories

In *True North: Discover Your Authentic Leadership,* Bill George and Peter Sims interviewed Howard Schultz, whose childhood story has defined his leadership:

"In the winter of 1961, seven-year-old Schultz was throwing snowballs with friends outside his family's apartment building in the federally

subsidized Bayview Housing Projects in Brooklyn, New York. His mother yelled down from their seventh-floor apartment, 'Howard, come inside. Dad had an accident.' What followed would shape him for the rest of his life.

He found his father in a full-leg cast, sprawled on the living room couch. While working as a delivery driver, he had fallen on a sheet of ice and broken his ankle. As a result, his father lost his job and the family's healthcare benefits. Worker's compensation did not yet exist, and his mother could not go to work because she was seven months pregnant. The family had nothing to fall back on. Many evenings, Schultz listened as his parents argued at the dinner table about how much money they needed to borrow and from whom. If the telephone rang, his mother asked him to answer it and tell the bill collectors his parents were not at home.

Schultz vowed he would do it differently when he had the opportunity. He dreamed of building a company that treated its employees well and provided healthcare benefits . . .

Memories of his father's lack of healthcare led Schultz to make Starbucks the first American company to provide access to health coverage for qualified employees who worked as little as twenty hours per week. 'My inspiration comes from seeing my father broken from the thirty terrible blue-collar jobs he had over his life, where an uneducated person just did not have a shot,' Schultz said.

His mother told him that he could do anything he wanted in America. 'From my earliest memories, I remember her saying that over and over again. It was her mantra.' His father had the opposite effect. As a truck driver, cab driver, and factory worker, he often worked two or three jobs at a time to make ends meet, but never earned more than $20,000 a year. Schultz watched his father break down as he complained bitterly about not having opportunities or respect from others.

As a teenager, Schultz felt the stigma of his father's failures, as the two clashed often. 'I was bitter about his underachievement and lack of responsibility,' he recalled. 'I thought he could have accomplished so much more if he had tried.' Schultz was determined to escape that fate. 'Part of *what has always driven me is fear of failure. I know all too well the face of self-defeat.*"[18]

Schultz's story perfectly illustrates that the stories we *choose* to believe win. Schultz could have chosen to believe, like his father did, that opportunities and respect from others would also elude him. He chose to believe his mother's side of the story—that he could do anything he wanted in America. Still, his father's misfortune became a catalyst for the type of company he could one day build. In the end, it came down to believing the right stories.

Bill George puts it best: "Although others may guide or influence you, your truth is derived from your life story and only you can determine what it should be." That's what Bridge Builders do—they *determine* what stories they should believe.

Don't Chuck Stories Born in the Parking Lot

Don't be surprised if the birth of a defining story takes place in unexpected places—even in the parking lot. That was the case for Facebook CEO Sheryl Sandberg, who opens *Lean In* with a story that took place during her tenure as a Google executive.

"One day, after a rough morning spent staring at the bottom of the toilet, I had to rush to make an important client meeting. Google was growing so quickly that parking was an ongoing problem, and the only spot I could find was quite far away. I sprinted across the parking lot, which in reality meant lumbering a bit more quickly than my absurdly slow pregnancy crawl. This only made my nausea worse, and I arrived at the meeting praying that a sales pitch was the only thing that would come out of my mouth. That night, I recounted these troubles to my husband, Dave. He pointed out that Yahoo, where he worked at the time, had designated parking for expectant mothers at the front of each building.

The next day, I marched in—or more like waddled in—to see Google founders Larry Page and Sergey Brin in their office . . . and announced that we needed pregnancy parking, preferably sooner rather than later. [Sergey] looked up at me and agreed immediately, noting that he had never thought about it before.

To this day, I'm embarrassed that I didn't realize that pregnant women needed reserved parking until I experienced my own aching feet. As one of Google's most senior women, didn't I have a special responsibility to think of this? But like Sergey, it had never occurred to me. The other pregnant women must have suffered in silence, not wanting to ask for special treatment. Or maybe they lacked the confidence or seniority to demand that the problem be fixed. Having one pregnant woman at the top—even one who looked like a whale—made a difference."[9]

At the core of Sandberg's story is the birth of newfound empathy for other women in the workplace—a story of empathy that promotes an attitude worth nurturing as a Bridge Builder Leader. It perfectly captures how believing a new story can shift how we lead.

Discovering Your Manifesto Stories

You may or may not be willing to share your Manifesto stories in the business world—at least not at first. More important is that you tell and retell these stories *to yourself.* Eventually you will find that being vulnerable to share certain stories will elevate your influence to new heights, because vulnerability leads to credibility. Until you are ready, your Manifesto stories are primarily for you—to transform the way you think, listen, act, communicate, and lead as a Bridge Builder. You'll know when sharing a particular story fits your audience, topic, and purpose.

So what type of stories should be part of your Bridge Builder Manifesto?

- Stories that inspire you to Think Like a Bridge Builder.
- Stories that inspire you to Listen Like a Bridge Builder.
- Stories that inspire you to Act Like a Bridge Builder.
- Stories that inspire you to Talk Like a Bridge Builder.
- Stories that inspire you to Lead Like a Bridge Builder.

When you examine Sandberg's and Schultz's stories, as well as the stories Daniel and Michael share in the parable, you'll notice that they fit several of the characteristics listed above.

Your Turn

Discovering and refining your Manifesto stories takes time—a lifetime in fact. As an executive coach, I find great satisfaction when I help leaders and teams discover and refine their Bridge Builder Manifesto stories. People from all walks of life—from engineers to executives, scientists to salespeople, teachers to pastors, housewives to college students—are positively transformed when they choose the Manifesto stories that set them apart as effective Bridge Builder leaders.

If you are committed to this process, you'll want to stop by the Book Resources Website to pick a copy of the Bridge Builder Manifesto Toolkit. It's a coaching tool I use to help leaders and teams discover and process stories that make their Bridge Builder Manifesto. It also will help you understand how to implement your Manifesto in business and home settings to increase your influence and effectiveness as a communicator and leader.

In the meantime, use the simplified approaches that follow to get you started. Remember that working on your Manifesto takes time and can be most effective with the help of a trusted coach or mentor who can help you point out blind spots and provide you with a more objective perspective.

The Organic Approach

You can discover defining stories in your life organically, every day— when you engage in meaningful conversation with someone who wants to learn about you *without agendas*. Yes, I know. That kind of empathy is rare today. In fact, when that happened to me I almost fell off my chair. A senior leader in the organization I was working for sent me an email that read—"Can we have coffee sometime next week? I'd love to know more about you and the journey you've been on . . ."

I showed up to our appointment properly cautious and suspicious, of course. But fifteen minutes into the conversation, I found myself sharing stories about my childhood I had forgotten and later realizing their influence on my leadership. I'm almost embarrassed to admit that one or two tears showed up in the conversation. But I'm grateful for insights that moment provided and how they have informed my authentic leadership.

If you have organic opportunities to unearth defining stories, then take the next step—intentionally process their influence by asking some of these questions:

- What has been the influence of this story in my personal and professional life?
- How has it influenced my character, mindset, and behavior?
- How has it affected my relationships?
- How has it affected my choices?
- How has it affected my ability to lead?
- Knowing what I know now, do these insights demand further action on my part?

The Smelly Rat Approach

Since stories we believe win, doesn't it make sense to find the stories *not* worth believing (the smelly rat)?

Consider Roger's example. I met him a year after he left his job as a marketing director for a small company to lead the marketing department of a much larger company. He had the credentials and the capacity to succeed. But after a year, his boss was concerned that members of his team were jumping ship, one by one, quickly.

In the process of looking for smelly rats, Roger recalled a story about his grandfather. As a government employee for over forty years, he had managed to care for his family, pay off his mortgage, and retire with a modest pension. His younger brother—the creative entrepreneur in the family—went bankrupt after losing several jobs. "He just couldn't learn to follow orders," his grandfather would say with scorn.

Roger didn't realize that his grandfather's stories had defined his contempt for independent-thinking creative types, like the smart creatives Schmidt and Rosenberg discuss in *How Google Works*. Roger found himself micromanaging them. One by one, members of his team were looking for the exit door because they couldn't work for someone who refused to listen to or trust his team.

Fortunately, Roger is turning things around—in larger part because he's taken the time to reframe the wrong stories by asking the hard questions:

- Why is this an important story?
- Why did I believe this story?
- Why is this story not true for me—given my unique set of circumstances?
- Is this story worth believing now—given what I know now?
- What do I gain by believing this story still?
- What do I lose by believing this story?
- How would my most trusted advisor (who knows me well) answer these questions on my behalf?
- Are there new facts or perspectives at my disposal that can help me reframe the story?
- Can I reframe the story, or is it time to let it go?

It's been my experience that everyone contends with at least one smelly rat. Take the time to hunt for pests that are robbing you of the satisfaction of leading yourself and others—effectively and authentically.

The Treasure Hunt Approach

The treasure hunt approach is a fun and rewarding exercise that leads you to search for the stories connected to your most rewarding choices and triumphs. When you find these stories, you realize that leadership is rooted in your core values and sense of purpose.

You can begin by writing down a story that answers some of these questions:

- What motivates you?
- Why do you do what you do?
- What scares you?
- What inspires you to face your fears and obstacles?
- Where did you learn to (insert Bridge Builder principle)?
- What made you choose your path, your business, and your direction?
- How did you overcome (insert a significant obstacle)?
- What gives you the resolve to keep moving forward?

When you invest time in harvesting your stories, the discoveries will surprise you.

Authentic leadership starts with one story. Bill George and Peter Sims, authors of *True North*, found this to be the case after interviewing 125 of today's top leaders—and it is true for you, too.

Trust the Process

I've met a number of leaders who dismiss the importance of harvesting Manifesto stories, because the process seems ambiguous or messy. If that's your first instinct, consider this simple advice—trust the process.

Think of your Manifesto as a living document. In fact, I recommend focusing on one story at a time. The Bridge Builder Manifesto Toolkit (available in the Resources Website) will further clarify how you can leverage the power of one story per year.

What's Your Bridge Builder Story?

I started this conversation with a bold assumption—*you already know how to be a Bridge Builder.* Somewhere along the way, you built a bridge to someone's heart and mind—and in the process you achieved something you wanted. Can you remember when it first happened? If you haven't already, it's time to remember that important story... and to connect the dots.

Allow me to illustrate with a personal example.

I was six, living in my native Mexico City. Student teachers from the college next to my school walked through my classroom door. Armed with enthusiasm and the latest technology of the day—color posters, glue, and glitter—they transformed first grade into the most creatively inspiring experience of my life.

When I got home that afternoon, I ran upstairs to find my dad and proceeded to deliver my first persuasive presentation with conviction and zeal: "Dad, I need to tell you why I want to be a teacher . . ."

The next day, I arrived home from school to find the spare room transformed into a charming classroom. A giant map of Mexico on one side of the wall, next to my new chalkboard. A little desk in the corner. Classic Dad. "You can achieve anything you want if you're willing to try."

And so with those words, every day after school, I ran to my little classroom and taught my students, a collection of stuffed animals, as well as my five-year old sister Corina.

My lessons consisted of everything I learned each morning at school.

Every day I drilled my class in vowel and consonant sounds. I showed my students how to shape their letters until they looked neat, all evenly shaped and evenly spaced. I taught them to add numbers forwards and backwards. And I told them all about Tenochtitlan, the place where the Aztecs built a beautiful city, which is now Mexico City.

Corina, my brightest student, came back day after day. She listened and raised her hand. She read her lessons and completed her math.

I was a good teacher!

By the end of that school year, the school principal called my parents to inform them that Corina should skip first grade. "She has learned how to read, write, and do first grade math as well as Maria can—she'll get bored in first grade," he said. And just like that, I lost my first real student. Teaching stuffed animals just wasn't the same.

It wasn't until many years later—after we lost Dad to brain cancer, after my family migrated to the United States, and after I learned enough English to enroll in my first college class—that I wrote about this story. I labored for weeks to write and rewrite an essay in response to the question, "Tell us why we should award you this college scholarship?" In the long, arduous, and intimidating journey to communicate my ideas for the first time—in writing, in English, and to an unfamiliar audience—a surprising revelation hit me: *I built a bridge!* I was only able to accomplish a dream because my audience—my father and my sister—embraced my ideas.

Then, a few weeks after I wrote the essay, I received an invitation to the annual banquet to honor both scholarship patrons and scholarship recipients.

After an inspiring keynote address, the time came to award the scholarships. One by one, the recipients were called to receive the awards. I rose and stepped onto the stage to receive mine, and the master of ceremonies and chair of the scholarship committee greeted me with a big smile. "You wrote a wonderful essay," she said as she shook my hand and handed me an envelope.

I thanked her and wondered if my astonishment showed on my face. *She remembers my essay and my name from among hundreds of applicants!* At that moment, I realized my story and words had moved the hearts of a scholarship committee. My story is memorable and my time investment to share it with authenticity and clarity has made *me* memorable to someone I've never met.

I built another bridge!

For the next four years, I rewrote the story to meet the criteria of each new scholarship committee. And little by little, I graduated from college debt-free—one story at a time, my barriers removed by the power of one bridge that connected me to my audience's heart.

I wish I could say that I never forgot the significance of that moment and the importance of being a Bridge Builder to achieve my dreams and goals. The truth is that I *did* forget. Not always. Mostly when it came to the most important goals and the most important relationships in my life. Sad, isn't it? Fortunately, it's never too late to repair damaged bridges or to build new ones. That has been my experience. That's what the Manifesto—this book—is all about.

It's never too late to reach for your most ambitious goals, and one story can put you on the right path.

What's your Bridge Builder story?

I know you have one. Remembering and examining that story will help you believe that you can do it again, today and tomorrow. The stories you believe win.

Let me sum up this section of the book by reiterating that your defining stories inform and inspire your authentic leadership—but you have to do the work to make sure the right stories are influencing the way you lead yourself and others.

Someone once said, "You are not born a winner. You are not born a loser. You are born a chooser."[20] Today you can choose to believe the right story—that you are a Bridge Builder and that you possess both the experience and the tools to build the bridges that lead to your goals and your dreams.

What are you waiting for?

CHAPTER 43

A CASE FOR BRIDGE BUILDER CULTURES

A few years ago, the Ken Blanchard Companies followed up on four different studies with a fifth study that aimed to understand the most critical components, skills, and mistakes connected to leadership. When more than 1400 leaders, managers, and executives were asked, "What is the biggest mistake leaders make when working with others?" Inappropriate use of communication/listening was cited as the number one mistake leaders make. [21]

This is a problem for most organizations. In short, inability or unwillingness to *build bridges* to the hearts and minds of stakeholders has big implications.

Investing in cultures where Bridge Builders can thrive has big implications too—the kind that positively affect the organization. I've seen it happen.

Ten years ago I arrived to San Diego to help deploy a new educational software solution across several academic organizations. The initiative involved one of those projects that the IT staff loved more than the end users. Change is always exciting for those who drive the change.

During the first two weeks, I launched a pilot program designed to implement this change, and it became immediately evident to me that two distinct groups of people were present in the organization: Bridge Builders and the rest of the group.

The latter group erected barriers by the mere fact that their focus was on tasks, timelines, and their own personal agendas, with little or no consideration for the needs of their respective audiences.

Bridge Builders, on the other hand, instinctively stepped into the role of advocates. They straddled the murky waters between those driving change and those whose work was disrupted by change. They listened more—whether they were on the side of mobilizing the change or on the receiving end. When possible, the Bridge Builders were willing to make modifications to their timelines or workflow for the good of those who would ultimately benefit from the initiative. They found ways to both motivate and negotiate. They were intentional about their attitudes and the way they communicated their plans and perspectives. Some of them even helped develop Blueprints that eventually simplified learning and execution for their peers.

Two years later, once this initiative was up and running smoothly, I proposed to pilot a new initiative that would leverage the lessons that had emerged from the previous experience. My assumption was that an intentional effort to nurture a culture of Bridge Builders would improve employee engagement and productivity across all the organizations— and so the Center for Excellence was born.

Akin to the parable's Center for Bridge Builder Leadership, the Center for Excellence became the catalyst for a culture where leaders and experts (and natural Bridge Builders) shared their expertise and their time in developing their peers, who in turn became Bridge Builders and shared their expertise and time developing their peers— and so on.

The model I followed was simple, cost effective, scalable, sustainable, and duplicable. The model boiled down to Principles, Tools, and Blueprints.

Engagement. This became the first and most evident return on investment—almost immediately. In fact, within the first year of the Center's operation, a group of about twenty-five employees, who were the most vocal champions of the Center for Excellence, raised well over ten thousand dollars in in-kind donations—and garnered the participation of dozens of additional strategic partners—to put together a weeklong leadership conference. And that was just the beginning.

Over time, it became evident that employees work harder, stay longer, and produce more when they are engaged, when they are developed, and when they feel successful.

This is only one example of the power of creating a Bridge Builder culture. People from engineers to salespeople, executives to entrepreneurs, parents to pastors have applied the principles in this book and ultimately received endorsements, approvals, funding, promotions, and more.

I've been privileged to witness that companies who nurture cultures of Bridge Builders (even if they don't use that name) are consistently rated among the "Best Companies to Work For" and report higher profits than their competitors.

Bottom line: Bridge Builders cultures achieve more.

A Bridge Builder culture starts with one champion—and that champion can be you!

CHAPTER 44

CHOOSE YOUR
ACTION PLAN

C atching the vision to be a Bridge Builder or to build a Bridge Builder Culture is the easy part. Keeping the vision alive is the challenge. Michael tells Daniel that vision leaks—the slow dissolution of the Bridge Builder culture—the reason why he takes drastic measures to make sure the vision remains alive in his organization. You may not be able to build a massive visual aid to keep the Bridge Builder Principles alive, like Michael does with his design of the MonikerTech campus, but you can keep the principles alive in creative ways. I offer three here and more in the Book Resources Website.

The Visual Action Plan

Simply put, implementing a Visual Action Plan involves adopting a strategy that keeps the Bridge Builder principles front and center in creative ways, so they gradually become part of the culture. For example, you can use the following graphic as a quick reference guide to help you and your team members remember the five Bridge Builder principles and most basic steps to live out each principle. Consider reviewing the

"Visual Aids" chapter of the parable with this image in hand. You can learn more about implementing a training strategy and find full color tools and visual aids at LeadersBuildBridges.com.

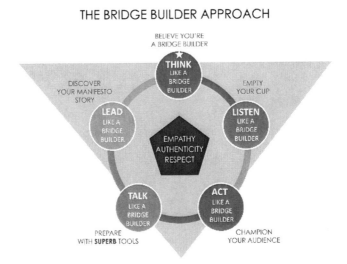

THE BRIDGE BUILDER APPROACH

- Discuss the significance of this image and how each element can serve as a reminder of Bridge Builder communication, leadership, attitudes, and best practices. Discussion questions can include:
- Which is the most crucial principle (the keystone habit that can trigger widespread change)?
- What does the triangle in the background indicate? Hint: think of the triangle as a funnel. When the bulk of your effort is spent at the top, the results are refined and flow down the rest of the principles.
- What can we do this week or month to keep (a chosen) principle alive?
- How can we make this principle tangible to our customers, partners, etc.?

Join the Bridge Builder Project: Read One, Share One

The Bridge Builder Project is an exciting initiative designed to inspire and facilitate one-on-one mentoring relationships in order to help team members succeed—in business and in life.

In short, you live out the parable in the book by becoming a Bridge Builder mentor to someone (inside or outside your organization) who desperately needs to become a Bridge Builder in order to achieve his or her dreams and goals. It's as simple as gifting a copy of the book to someone you'd like to mentor and then inviting that individual to meet on a regular basis to discuss the parable and the principles. In the process, mentoring paths will emerge, and you will be able to guide your mentee through the principles, best practices, and tools that will make real impact.

Along the way, you will also benefit as you gain valuable insights that will make you an even more successful Bridge Builder. As the old adage says, "The best way to learn is to teach."

Individuals and organizations can join the Bridge Builder Project at **LeadersBuildBridges.com** and download free learning and coaching resources.

Bring a "Bridge Builders in a Box" Event to Your Organization

"Bridge Builders in a Box" is a turnkey event that brings all the Bridge Builder inspiration and training to your organization with minimal preparation on your part. Whether it's a company-wide conference or an intimate leadership retreat—a Bridge Builders event can be the catalyst you need to:

- Introduce or communicate change with a powerful themed event
- Pilot a Bridge Builder organizational initiative
- Develop your leaders under a unified vision
- Build teamwork around specific projects or initiatives
- Deliver customized training to improve customer service, presentations, meetings, etc.

**Learn more and download a flyer at
LeadersBuildBridges.com.**

Whatever you decide to do—be intentional and make sure your new vision doesn't leak!

SUPPLEMENTAL RESOURCES

If you are interested in bringing a Bridge Builder Program to your organization, Maria and her team conduct lunch and learn sessions, leadership retreats, on-site and online training, executive coaching, train-the-trainer workshops, team-building sessions, and "Bridge Builders in a Box" event packages for all types of organizations.

In addition, **LeadersBuildBridges.com** houses the resources listed below, designed to help you and your team continue growing as Bridge Builder communicators and leaders.

The SUPERB Assessment is a strategic feedback collection tool you can take for yourself and share with your peers to gather valuable information about how you come across as a communicator. It measures how your attention to Story, Usefulness, Passion, Empathy, Reliability, and Brevity maximizes or minimizes the effectiveness of your message.

The Bridge Builder Manifesto Toolkit is a coaching tool to help you discover and refine the personal stories that help you lead more authentically.

Additional resources include:

- Personal Bridge Builders Action Plan
- Discussion Guides:
    - Bridge Builders at Home
    - Bridge Builders at School
    - Bridge Builders at Church
    - Bridge Builders in Sales
    - Bridge Builders in Healthcare
- Articles and interviews with influential Bridge Builders leaders
- Templates and Blueprints for Business Communication
- VIP access to new tools and resources as they become available

---

Web: LeadersBuildBridges.com
Email: maria@LeadersBuildBridges.com
Twitter: @MariaKeckler

ACKNOWLEDGMENTS

Writing—at least for me—is a painful, yet exhilarating collaborative process, wrought with anxiety, false starts, discovery, stops, and beginnings anew. Bridge Builders like you made it impossible for me to quit when that's all I wanted to do.

Thank you . . .

For inspiring me to start. Pam Farrel, for being the first one to say—"I hope one day you write a leadership book." Bob Murtha, Kevin Clark, Linda Halisky, David Gillette, and Robert Webber—for challenging me, teaching me, and pushing me to think and write like a Bridge Builder before I knew better.

For shaping my perspective. Patrick Lencioni, Drs. Ken and Marjorie Blanchard, Seth Godin, Nancy Duarte, Michael Hyatt, Dr. Brené Brown, Annette Simmons, Diane West, Mary Ann Mariani, Andy Stanley, Joyce Tepfer, and Dr. David Jeremiah. Your words, your leadership, and your generosity have inspired my work and my life.

For helping me cross the finish line. Melissa Carson Thomas, David Thomas, Lisa Gates, Thomas Varallo, Kathy King, Holly Abeel, Jesse Abeel, J.D. Davids, Kathy Leicester, Jennifer Dryer-Patton, Donna Evans, Stan Evans, Tom Stoyan, Geoffrey Berwind, Martha Bullen, Steve Harrison, Beth Moseley, Mike Lopez, and Diane Szuch—for applauding, researching, reading, proofreading, providing feedback, or sharing your stories with me. Without your help, support, and contribution, this book would not be a reality.

Shelly Beach, my editor and friend, you held my hand as I struggled through dozens of drafts and restarts—and taught me to be a better storyteller without sacrificing the integrity of my voice. You're a terrific teacher. I sound better because of you!

For believing—always. My beloved family—Mom, Manny, Corina, Jennifer, and Daniel—for believing, praying, and walking with me—at every turn.

Sarah, you inspire me to be a better Bridge Builder.

Sam, without your unwavering strength, selflessness, love, support, wisdom, feeding and watering—nothing would ever come to fruition. We succeed together!

For who I am, who I'm becoming, and what I'm able to do. God—my father, my friend, my savior, and my guide. May all I do be pleasing to you, Jesus, The Bridge Builder of my heart.

ABOUT THE AUTHOR

 Maria Keckler is on a mission to transform organizations into Bridge Builder cultures where people show up every day excited to make a difference—even to change the world—one conversation, one meeting, one project, one relationship, one presentation, one initiative, and one story at a time.

An educator at heart, Maria is an international speaker, author, and founder of Superb Communication, a San Diego-based firm specializing in strategic communication solutions, executive coaching, and training.

As a consultant and strategic partner, Maria works with companies to transform organizational cultures and to develop, advance, and retain top talent.

In one-on-one coaching, team facilitation, workshops, and keynote presentations, Maria helps professionals deliver more compelling presentations, facilitate more productive and creative meetings, communicate more effectively during change, and craft powerful stories that improve business results.

Maria's experience spans almost twenty years, developing and coaching global leaders across the United States, Mexico, and Eastern Europe. She's worked with executives, engineers, scientists, educators, and leaders in healthcare, pharmaceuticals, biotechnology, communication, technology, education, and the non-profit sector.

Maria is an avid student of leadership and communication. She studied English, linguistics, and technical communication at Cal Poly, San Luis Obispo, where she earned bachelor's and master's degrees. She lives in San Diego with Sam, her business partner and husband of twenty-eight years, and their daughter, Sarah.

NOTES

The parable is a fictional story inspired by composites of real people I've worked with—not anyone in particular. If at any point you found yourself saying, "I know Daniel!" or "I'm Daniel..." you are in good company.

1 Duhigg, Charles. *The Power of Habit: Why We Do what We Do in Life and Business.* New York: Random House, 2012.
2 Duarte, Nancy. *HBR Guide to Persuasive Presentations.* Boston, MA: Harvard Business Review Press, 2012.
3 Lencioni, Patrick. *The Five Dysfunctions of a Team: A Leadership Fable.* San Francisco: Jossey Bass, 2002.
4 Tagore, Rabindranath. Quoted by Mel Gussow. "THINK TANK; Is Truth True? Or Beauty? A Couple of Thinkers Go Deep." *The New York Times.* Accessed September 03, 2014, http://www.

nytimes.com/2001/08/18/arts/think-tank-is-truth-true-or-beauty-a-couple-of-thinkers-go-deep.html.

5   "Tony Hsieh: 'I Fire Those Who Don't Fit Our Company Culture' [VIDEO]." Inc.com. Accessed September 2014, http://www.inc.com/allison-fass/tony-hsieh-zappos-i-fire-non-culture-fits-fast.html?nav=pop.

6   Blanchard, Ken. "Twitted by @KenBlanchard." December 5, 2013.

7   Stanley, Andy. "The Art of Inviting Feedback Part I and II." *Andy Stanley Leadership Podcast*, November 4 and December 9, 2013. Accessed November 09, 2014, http://podbay.fm/show/290055666.

8   Schank, Robert C. Quoted by Daniel H. Pink in *A Whole New Mind: Why Right-brainers Will Rule the Future*. New York: Riverhead Books, 2006.

9   Smith, Paul. *Lead with a Story: A Guide to Crafting Business Narratives That Captivate, Convince, and Inspire*. New York: American Management Association, 2012.

10 Geoffrey Berwind. Quoted by Roger D. Duncan. "Tap the Power of Storytelling." *Forbes*. Accessed October 08, 2014, http://www.forbes.com/sites/rodgerdeanduncan/2014/01/04/tap-the-power-of-storytelling/.

11 Simmons, Annette. *The Story Factor: Secrets of Influence from the Art of Storytelling*. Cambridge, MA: Perseus Pub., 2001.

12 Giannetto, David F. *Big Social Mobile: How Digital Initiatives Can Reshape the Enterprise and Drive Results*. New York: Palgrave MacMillan, 2014.

13 Gentry, William A., Toy J. Webber, and Golnaz Sadri. "Empathy in the Workplace: A Tool for Effective Leadership." April 2007. Accessed November 2, 2014, http://www.ccl.org/Leadership/pdf/research/EmpathyInTheWorkplace.pdf.

14 Southwest Airlines. "Southwest Heart." Accessed December 07, 2014, http://www.southwest-heart.com/.

15 Zappos.com, Powered by Service. "Zappos Family Core Values." Accessed August 07, 2014, http://about.zappos.com/our-unique-culture/zappos-core-values.

16 Schmidt, Eric, Jonathan Rosenberg, and Alan Eagle. *Google: How Google Works*. New York: Grand Central Publishing, 2014.

17 Brown, Brené. "The Power of Vulnerability." TED. Accessed April 08, 2014, http://www.ted.com/talks/brene_brown_on_vulnerability.

18 George, Bill, and Peter Sims. *True North: Discover Your Authentic Leadership*. San Francisco, CA: Jossey-Bass/John Wiley & Sons, 2007.

19 Sandberg, Sheryl, and Nell Scovell. *Lean In: Women, Work, and the Will to Lead*. New York: Knopf, 2013.

20 Anonymous. Quoted by Michael Hyatt. Accessed August 07, 2014, http://michaelhyatt.com/quotes/you-are-born-a-chooser.

21 The Ken Blanchard Companies. "Critical Leadership Skills: Key Traits That Can Make or Break Today's Leaders (Research Findings)." Accessed April 08, 2014. http://www.kenblanchard.com/img/pub/pdf_critical_leadership_skills.pdf